From New York to Vancouver

Stories on the Fly

ALSO AVAILABLE:

My Schizophrenic Life: The Road to Recovery from Mental Illness by Sandra Yuen MacKay

Chop Shtick by Sandra Yuen MacKay

Bounty Hunter by Jonathan Marsh and James D. Young

Time Passages by James D. Young

RERUN by James D. Young

Boulevard by James D. Young

From New York to Vancouver

Stories on the Fly

By

Sandra Yuen MacKay and James D. Young

From New York to Vancouver
Copyright © 2018 Sandra MacKay and James D. Young

Untitled Story
Copyright © 2018 Sandra MacKay and James D. Young

Legacy
Copyright © 2012 James D. Young
Reprinted from *Time Passages*, 2012

Inner Circle
Copyright © 2018 Sandra MacKay

Cover photos and design
Copyright © 2018 by Sandra MacKay

All rights reserved. The use of any part of this publication reproduced, transmitted in any form or by any means, mechanical, digital, photocopying, recording or otherwise, without the prior consent of the author, is an infringement of the Copyright Laws.

First Edition
March, 2018

Printed by CreateSpace
Charleston, SC

ISBN-13: 978-1979805346
ISBN-10: 1979805342

Dedication

To romances all over the globe…

To my dear husband and family
- Sandra Yuen MacKay

&

For my longtime friend, Will "Sugarfoot" Hutchins,
and his ever-lovely wife Babs
- James D. Young

Contents

Untitled Story   9
by Sandra Yuen MacKay and James D. Young

Legacy   121
by James D. Young

Inner Circle   139
by Sandra Yuen MacKay

Untitled Story

By

Sandra Yuen MacKay and James D. Young

1.

I've never remotely considered myself a writer, but the prose of modern masters has captivated me ever since high school. From Ernest Hemingway to J.D. Salinger. From Sinclair Lewis to Jack Kerouac. From William Faulkner to Stephen King. Whatever excess funds were available went for books. Of course, I'd learned early on to avoid the hacks and formula-driven no-talents of both genders who manage to sell copies of their drivel by the millions and who will deservedly go unnamed here. Public taste often seems to reside in its oral cavity.

Last night as I relaxed with "Western Wall/The Tucson Sessions," a rare, late '90s CD of uncommon excellence by Linda Ronstadt and Emmylou Harris, I found myself exploring literary sites on the Internet. A favorite is Wordsmiths.net on which I relish the solid writing by talented professionals and amateurs alike. I jumped to the New Entries section where I found myself captivated and swept along by a newcomer, at least to my knowledge.

Her byline was Samantha Chu. If not a pseudonym, I'd be forced to guess she's Chinese. Asian, at the very least. She'd posted the first chapter of a new novel entitled *The Boy Who Got Away*. By the end of the first section, heavily steeped in Eastern culture and family life, I was so entranced by her story and style that I bade adieu to the two divas and switched the CD player over to my beloved "Phases of the Moon," traditional Chinese music, for heightened effect.

As Miss Chu seductively described the early home life of her characters, I was drawn into that west coast household, a captive spectator. When she described hurt, I felt it. If she related a humorous anecdote, I found myself unconsciously laughing. But this had to be fiction because no person alive could do this kind of justice to an autobiography.

The woman could do no wrong in that first chapter, but upon its conclusion, I felt like a junkie strung out for his next fix. Would there be more? There were no comments posted for her, despite the story's being up there for an entire week. Hot damn, I *have* to be the first to write.

An unusual case of nerves, however, prevented me from doing anything at that moment.

I couldn't get her well-crafted tale out of my head at work the next day. Mental phrases danced around and worked their way through my loopy brain, but none of it was work-related. All day long my co-workers kept giving me strange sideways looks. Especially Lucy, the dark-skinned Mexican femme fatale with her glaring devil's eyes, complete with piercing, dagger-like eyebrows. Occasional glances from her and others, yes, but they were all unnerving. I couldn't wait until I was home again, safe within the haven of my bachelor's pad.

Stopping later that evening at a local supermarket after another maddening rush hour commute aboard the subway, I picked up a frozen meal. Chicken Kiev. It would be a filling, tasty and quick-to-prepare meal that would not delay my returning to the Wordsmiths website.

After dinner, I noticed my palms were perspiring. But why? I'd given writers occasional online feedback before, both the positive and negative variety. I was uncertain of her writing background, despite a fluid proficiency with the language, but I found my comments were barely half-prepared. There was lingering trepidation in my fingers as I began to fidget in my chair. Hardly a fast typist, I've always used what has been referred to by some as the Biblical Method: "Seek and ye shall find."

A drink was also definitely in order. A man who feels a bit indecisive sometimes needs a fast belt to bolster his resolve. A Smirnoff Vodka and Mountain Dew with a twist of lime would do the trick. I hoped, anyway.

Before considering an opening sentence, I re-read the chapter in its entirety. Twice. Now I was hooked. Hopelessly addicted. But, I had to tell myself, it was also time to be brave. Still, my two fingers seemed to twitch slightly as I typed the following:

After reading your first chapter several times yesterday and this evening, Ms. Chu, I felt compelled to enter a comment or three on your story and very evident talent.

I am not a writer, but an avid reader, so it is a skill to draw a youthful east coast man into such a story gently laced with Asian culture. When you mentioned those red envelopes given during the Lunar New Year, it reminded me of a Vietnamese family I'd known who did that for Tet each year. It brought back sweet memories of the time I had purchased a small packet of them and placed a dollar bill in each for their children. I'll never forget their smiles.

I'm quite curious as to whether there will be a follow-up chapter of your novel posted on Wordsmiths in the near future. If that is your intent, then I look forward to it. If not, I'll have to exercise some super-human patience and be the first in line at my neighborhood bookstore in Greenwich Village to purchase it when it is eventually published.

    I needed a refill for my drink. Colder, this time. Whole lots colder. My mouth was parched. Would she think I was fawning over her work? Did my note ring false or come across as overly complimentary? Would she even consider replying? I didn't know, but I reviewed it one last time just in case before adding, "Best regards and good luck from Peter Petrovich." Then I double-checked my often-crappy spelling before pressing the key to send my message.
    The proverbial ball was now about to land on Samantha Chu's side of the court...

2.

I woke up with a headache the size of Manhattan. I don't know why I had New York on my mind, as I was located on the west coast, a twenty-year-old Vancouverite living in British Columbia. Certainly I'd never been to the Big Apple. I hadn't been farther east than Toronto to visit relatives who never invited us back after my mom called my uncle "Attila the Hun" on account of his short stature and beard and his tendency to slap his kids anytime they got out of line. Aunt Hilary didn't like us either after Dad went down to the wine cellar and helped himself to an expensive bottle of rare Chardonnay and proceeded to knock over the wine rack accidentally, breaking about ten bottles of wine. Miraculously the Scotch was saved, but Attila was ready to hang Dad. Aunt Hilary called a taxi to take us to the airport and practically chased us out the door with her son's hockey stick. My cousin Stevie was obese, but could skate like the wind. I predicted he had a great future as a pro hockey player or bouncer at the local bar. Take your pick.

As a teenager, I did visit the island of Oahu about five years ago. Too young to drink Mai Tais and too old to hang out at the kiddie pool. My parents kept an eye on me so I couldn't even flirt with any of the blond surfer guys at Waikiki beach. I returned home sun-dried the colour of sockeye salmon. I peeled so badly that I felt like an onion.

On another occasion, our family went to Disneyland, a rite of passage for any kid growing up in North America. Mostly what I remember from that vacation is a bad tummy ache from too much candy and severe motion sickness. I avoid lollipops to this day because they remind me of the six suckers I ate before I puked on the Matterhorn. One of those memories you wish would disappear faster than bad credit.

Sitting down in front of my computer with a cup of freshly brewed java, I clicked on Wordsmiths.net, hoping for a response to the first chapter of *The Boy Who Got Away*. The impetus for the story had hit me like a bolt of lightning. In fact, I was blow-drying my hair and received an electric shock from an exposed wire when the plot suddenly flashed before my eyes like a movie revealed in a millisecond. I put pen to paper and wrote nonstop for six weeks. It sounds like a cliché to say it wrote itself, but it did. I believed there was a reason I wrote it. Cause and effect. Call me psychic.

* * *

I scanned the computer screen for my post, but I didn't have my hopes up too high that anyone even noticed the chapter was there. Even a negative comment was better than nothing. Critics online can be harsh. It comes with the territory.

To my amazement, there was a comment from someone named Peter Petrovich. What kind of name was that? I was intrigued. He said that he lived in Greenwich Village. Wasn't I just thinking about New York? I noted he was familiar with *lycee*, an Asian custom of giving. Who was he? A Croatian anthropologist of Chinese customs? My mouth dropped when he said he'd like to purchase my book. I had a fan!

Deciding to send him a private message on Wordsmiths.net, I began to type.

Dear Peter,

Thanks for the response to my post. I feared no one would comment at all. Or someone would tell me to get a real job and give up writing altogether. Actually, I'm a college student studying general arts, which basically means I don't know what the hell I'm doing because I can't choose a major. I am the epitome of indecision in regards to a career. That's why I write. To help me release the fear of uncertainty around my life. Do you have any idea of how hard it is to get a job that pays well when one has no marketable skills? Actually, I do have some skills in the areas of procrastination and spelling. Isn't that a wonderful combination? Anybody in need of a lazy proofreader who can't meet deadlines? See what I mean?

Are you a collector? The reason I ask is because sometimes I have premonitions about people. I can't get a read on what you look like, but I definitely sense rows of books and music CDs.

- Just Curious Samantha

3.

TGIF.

If I can get through this final, stinking workday unscathed and remain unruffled, I might find myself enjoying a better-than-average weekend. Could be. No solid date lined up, but one never knows. Hey, it happened to Ernest Borgnine in *Marty*, that old classic, although it took him the whole blasted movie to get up the nerve to stand up against his lowlife "pals" and ask her out.

The spring weather has been fresh and invigorating, despite a lingering nip in the air from "The Winter That Wouldn't Quit." This season traditionally presages rebirth and renewal. First Easter and the Resurrection. Flowers and the grass. Then us. In that order. It has always been so. What's the old saying? "In the springtime when a young man's fancy turns to thoughts of...sex."

Yeah, they sure got *that* right.

With no real pressing need for direct deposit, I cashed my paycheck at the bank during the lunch hour and deposited about half. I felt more surprised than gratified to see some of my savings actually accruing for a change. A thought has been crossing my mind to convert some of it into one of those Certificates of Deposit to yield a higher interest rate. I'll give it serious consideration, provided the goddamned landlord doesn't jack up my rent again.

Back at my desk, I stared at the spreadsheets on my computer screen. Bor-ing. But that's what they pay me for. With a mental image of my two overbearing bosses in mind, the guy as ruthless as Genghis Khan, and the nasty middle-aged woman who should have a bumper sticker that reads "MY OTHER CAR IS A BROOM," I smiled as I raised my middle finger to the PC screen and said aloud, "Analyze this."

Come Christmas, I might even consider soliciting the staff for contributions to buy her a personality transplant at Bellevue.

"Hey, Pete," said Johnny the mail clerk, sticking his disheveled head into my tiny office cubicle, "we're going on a Starbucks run at 2:30. You in the mood for one?"

I reached for my wallet.

"Yeah, a grande Al Cappuccino would go down perfect. And

tell the barista lots of foam and sugar. Thanks loads, pal."

It was just the right diversion for me to switch mental gears from spreadsheets to Ms. Samantha Chu and her enticing tale. I wonder whether she had read my comments and, if she had, did she deem them worthy of a response? I glanced at my watch – mere hours before I ditched this bullshit office façade and did battle with the hordes on the evening rush hour aboard the grimy downtown local #6 subway train back to the Bleecker Street station in the Village.

* * *

Home Sweet Pad.

The first thing I did was to get my computer into operation. Why does it take so long to load the same stupid programs that I use every single day? Gates' Merry Band of Grammarians should be drawing unemployment for all they don't know about spelling, syntax, grammar and the English language in general. "It's" is "it is," *not* a flipping possessive. And the dolts always mistake a subordinate clause for a fragment. Look for subject and verb, you morons! Jeez.

"Syntax."

Those nerds probably think it's a surcharge on you-know-what.

But I guess they don't get much of that. "Selfie," a current trendy term, takes on a brand new significance for those clowns. Handy – if one catches my not-so-subtle drift. Wankers, all...

My less-than-nimble fingers typed in the Wordsmiths site. After logging in, I saw my comment to Samantha Chu, but no reply from her. My heart more or less sank – until I noticed a small icon flashing at the bottom, alerting me to a private message. I clicked on it, and a message popped up. Hey, it was from Samantha! I read it with eagerness. It was general, and certainly cordial enough, but with several surprises. She was a *college student* – and majoring in nothing? How could a writer of such depth be so youthful? I'd fully expected her to be much closer in age to my thirty years. Maybe even older. Life experiences and all that rot.

Anyway, it was deserving of an instant reply. To prevent a

case of forgetfulness, I jotted a few key notes on a pad next to the keyboard before answering her.

Take two deep breaths, I commanded myself, and begin typing...

Hello, Samantha ~

Thank you for replying so promptly to my comments on your outstanding first chapter. I meant what I said about enjoying it, and I hope there will be more soon.

You're a procrastinator also? My lifelong motto has been: "Never put off until tomorrow what you can put off indefinitely."

I must ask: Are you psychic? Me – a collector? That's funny. I think I'm far more of a hoarder than a collector. Well, my dad did dabble in coins and stamps, but I always found those hobbies less than engrossing. I need something much more sensory – things for the mind, the ears and the eyes. So you're right on the money about books and music. Movies, too. Some old, some foreign. My space in this high-priced flat is fairly limited, so I find myself going to Home Depot to buy supplies to build wall units complete with shelving for my many CDs and DVDs.

As for the books, I keep only those that have meant much to me over the years. The rest I sell over at Strand Books near Union Square. They buy used ones for their very large clientele, a never-ending stream of casual shoppers, tourists and diehard bibliophiles. Trouble is, the staff doesn't pay much. I had an oversized Rizzoli book ($75 new) on the films of Kurosawa. They only gave me five dollars in credit, but when I spotted it for sale in the front window the next week, it was marked at $40. I guess their overhead in this expensive city is damned high, too.

Enough about me. Getting work is tough all over. Since I am quite clueless regarding the geographical location where you call home, I can't advise you on any trends or openings. What I can tell you is that you have considerable skills as a writer. From your opening sentence and beyond, you had this boy hooked. Have you spoken with a counselor at your university or tried to have smaller pieces (like brief essays or poems) published in the student magazine, if they have one? What kind of newspapers are in your area? Do they feature straight reporting, or do they sometimes run op-ed items, including letters to the editor? Real easy to get your name out there, especially with your keen sense of humor. And don't forget blogging. Everyone else in the world seems to have their very own blog these days. Yours could be quite unique.

Look, I hope this doesn't sound forward of me. I rarely do this, but here's my e-mail addy if you should wish to drop me an occasional note about your writing progress. Better than relying on the dubious privacy of some literary website:

PetersPet30@yahoo.com.

4.

Howdie Peter,

You are not the only one to get taken by a used bookstore. It gives new meaning to the phrase "read it and weep."

You mention you are a hoarder? There's a reality TV show about that if you should ever need someone to clean up your place. They send in people with masks who throw out all your belongings, including pets, food and anything left on the floor. One man's trash is another man's treasure as the saying goes.

There's a lot to be said for wall units. They have nice cubbyholes for not only CDs and DVDs, but also for my Peanuts collection of porcelain figurines. I, for one, love IKEA for low cost, do-it-yourself furniture. I'm sure there's one in New York.

I go to college in Vancouver, British Columbia, which has their own newspaper published by the journalism department. But I don't think the editor is going to publish anything that I've written in the school newspaper anytime soon, because I met him in the cafeteria without knowing who he was and accidentally spilled Caesar salad and a soft drink on his linen shirt. That caused him to knock his tablet off the table. When I leaned over to say I was sorry, I stepped on his tablet, shattering the screen with a spiked heel.

I tried to apologize again, but he told me to crawl into a dumpster where I belong. Now I don't have anything against dumpster divers per se or people who do sleep in dumpsters for warmth, but I was damn offended, so I told him that he couldn't tell the difference between garbage and his brain. After that, a woman interrupted and said, "Don't you know who he is? He's the editor of the college newspaper."

I gulped, realizing my *faux pas* of *faux pas*. "Oh, my name is Samantha Chu," I said. "Did you get the poem I submitted? I was hoping to get it published." My face flushed with embarrassment. My knees felt weak like toothpicks holding me up.

The editor sneered. "Think again, Miss Chu. Your poem will never see the light of day." His eyes narrowed and he gave a

haughty laugh, which I will never forget.
    Well, enough about me.
    If you want to email me, just reply to this address.

Signing off,
Samantha the Smart-Ass

5.

I was stunned by the klutzy revelations in Samantha's first direct e-mail to my inbox. How does one who writes so well manage to self-destruct so effectively in real life? Like her screwing up any chance she had with an editor to get published? This was beyond me. Unless she's just putting me on. That's always a possibility. It's not all that unusual for total strangers online to adopt masks and poses to keep people off-balance and guessing.

If not, however, should I offer her some brotherly advice or toss her a life preserver? That'd be the latent social worker in me talking. My late mom used to say something like that. Perhaps I should gently back off before terminating any and all future correspondence with her. I was confused. I needed to think about what a potential can of worms I'd opened in haste and with such enthusiasm. Christ, I don't even know what this college babe looks like. If she should be an Ugly Duckling, no biggie, but what if she's drop-dead gorgeous? That'd be one sick joke on me, right? Inside my head I began to hear snippets of a Bob Seger song, "Beautiful Loser."

Her – or me?

I shut off the damn PC and went food shopping to clear my head.

Several hours and two days later, nothing seemed to be working. It has taken me a full week before resigning myself to send her another e-mail...and with a decided shift in tone and relative lack of interest. Would she pick up on that? Or just take it at face value?

Only time will tell...

Hello, Samantha ~

Overtime has exhausted me lately. No time or energy to go online. Sorry about that.

So, you're Canadian. Well, being on the other side of this large continent, there's no chance to share a cup of coffee with you, is there? That's a shame.

Your quote in my neighborhood would be "One man's trash is another man's garbage." There are so many of those "dumpster divers" you mentioned, along with hopeless "bag people" and homeless folks hanging out hereabouts. While at Strand, I noticed that they had two full seasons of A&E's "Hoarders" on sale for $10 for each DVD set. Despite being totally unfamiliar with that particular show, I passed on buying either because I'm not really all that bad. Anyhow, it's time for spring cleaning for this accumulator. Goodbye to clutter. And without wearing a mask.

Yes, we do have an Ikea, quite popular, located in a section of Brooklyn's waterfront. Regarding your "Peanuts collection," did you mean very tiny items or figures of characters like Snoopy, Lucy, Linus and Charlie Brown from that old comic strip? Just a guess.

Apologies for a rather short note, but I have many work assignments to complete on deadline.

Take care.

Peter

6.

I sensed a distinct change in tone in Peter's emails. First charm and then a rather cooler response. Curiously, he was similar to me in that respect. My moods changed as quickly as clicking TV channels on a remote. Maybe he was turned off by my email. I hadn't presented my best side, but it wasn't like it was a job interview at Microsoft. Or maybe I was reading too much into his message. Perhaps he was busy like he said, but at least he made an effort to write.

As I looked out the window at the rain, I wondered about his life, job, or if he had a wife or children. Pete was more complicated than I originally thought, but I really didn't know much about him based on a few emails. He was apologetic, but I thought something was going on with him. With my sixth sense, I figured he didn't have a hidden agenda and was a normal type of guy. He was right we weren't going for coffee anytime soon, but perhaps we could have an intelligent conversation, which was rare in my circles. I wrote back, starting with a question.

Forgive my curiosity, but are you leery of me? Because I feel the same way. The Internet is full of scam artists or people pretending to be someone they aren't.

Not to worry. I'm not a hag with a missing tooth and I don't practice witchcraft. I eat with a fork and have cream in my coffee. I dream of visiting Paris and Rome, but can barely afford a bus pass. And I also have a few collectible items. You asked about it, and your second answer was correct. My collection consists of porcelain models that are sculptures of Peanuts characters in various actions. You can Google: Peanuts Porcelain Hallmark.

I saw a career counselor and he asked me what I wanted to do with my life. "What do I not want to do?" I replied. Being twenty years old, I should be enjoying a full life, but instead I feel caught in a maze. Do you ever feel like that?

Just to let you know, the editor of the newspaper was fired for absconding with funds and spending the money on ladies he found online and Kokanee. I read about him being fired in the gossip column of the college newspaper. I didn't figure him to be a womanizer with a drinking problem, but you never know what secrets people carry. I didn't pick up on it because he's a smoker. My ESP doesn't work with people that smoke, strangely enough.

Kelly Mason is the new editor. She's about five foot two with blue hair and chews gum a lot. I needed to know what she looks like before I spill food on her by accident. (I'm joking.) I dropped off an article at her office and shook her hand. Sometimes when you shake someone's hand, you get a sense of them. She seems honest enough. There's hope for me yet! Fingers crossed she'll like my article – how computers have made my generation into low-grade spellers. There's a reason for paper and pen. People need to know how to write without Spellcheck.

Another piece of good news is I had my loan approved for school which will pay for my tuition to the end of next term. My dad said that I need to get a part-time job. So he spoke to his friend, a manager at a local drugstore to see if I could get a job at the cosmetics counter. I have an interview next week. Wow! Good things happen in threes! I never thought of myself as a make-up artist, but I do know how to read the labels on mascara.

Would you like me to send you the manuscript of my novel? If you wait for me to post chapters on Wordsmiths.net, it'll be a long time before the conclusion. I'd really appreciate your reading it if you were interested and could give me some feedback. Pretty please?

Best to you,
Samantha, Writer on the loose

7.

After I'd sent that e-mail to Samantha last week, I felt pretty damned wretched. She had done nothing to upset me, so why the hell was I so put off? Maybe it was a form of misdirected anger over the day I'd been having. But as soon as I received her reply, the dark skies seemed to dissipate and brighten. Perhaps I could answer her questions and put her at ease, so I plopped myself in front of the PC and started tapping away at the keys like a man possessed...

Hello, Loose & Leery Writer ~

If you had known what kind of day I'd put in when I last wrote you, you'd understand a bit better how life in the Big Bad Apple can eat one up alive. One of my bosses had been all over my sorry butt from start to finish. Wire-to-wire, as they say in O. Henry's horse-racing circles. You should remember – always – that boss spelled backwards is double s-o-b. But some future day I'll exact a fitting measure of revenge. For right now, please just write off my less-than-enthusiastic note as a kind of male version of PMS. Fair enough? OK, then. Onward.

I'm doing a happy dance (from Charlie Schultz's dog in "Peanuts") over your request to send the full manuscript of your novel. I've noticed you've had six additional comments posted by others on Wordsmith.net, and all favorable. Not a disparaging note in sight. So many thanks in advance for sending it. Provided, of course, you've already had it copyrighted in Canada. I can promise you only one thing: honesty. I'll try to provide the most objective critique while occasionally correcting spelling or catching typos. Because of my all-too-often goofy schedule, I'll send along my comments in installment fashion, if that's acceptable to you.

I fully agree that there are many scammers and posers online. I don't like them much either, but to make you feel less leery that I could be one of them, let's play a variation on "20 Questions." I'll start it off to make it easier for you later on.

I'm a lifelong non-smoker. (Non-toker, too.) So no smokescreens to fog up your ESP.

I'm past you in age by a full decade. (But is anyone out there counting? Does anyone even care?) That's what the "30" in my e-addy means. But if I sound older at times, you can blame it on the closeness I had with dad. We tended to think alike most of the time. But trust me. I really am 30.

As for the "s," I wanted it to be Peter's Pet, but the carrier doesn't allow for punctuation. One of my father's old school textbooks had a sticker that read: "Teachers Pet – So Do Others." When I couldn't use the apostrophe, I made it stand for my middle name, Sergei. Russian heritage. (And no "Sir Gay" rainbow jokes allowed. Just flashback to the recent Winter Olympics and think of Putin's hard-line stance on them.)

Never been married. A bachelor by definition: "A guy with no children...to speak of." LOL.

But I did live with a gal for about a year a while back. Beyond obvious availability and sexual attraction, there was no other glue holding us together. When we later woke up to the realization that we were getting bored in a one-dimensional, dead-end situation, we mutually decided to go our separate ways and to search for more suitable pastures out there in the real world.

As for family, I have a brother, Damir. (I've always called him "Damn," much to the chagrin of my red-faced parents, both gone now.) He's five years my junior and lives much closer to you out on the west coast – in Oakland, CA. Damir's one of those brainy types who slaves his life away in a nerdy Neverland known as Silicon Valley. (I tell him it's really "Silicone" Valley in the event he wants to develop a bigger, manlier chest.) It's been a few years since we've seen each other, so I'm giving serious thought to flying out there on my vacation next summer.

As for Paris? Rome? Let's book a flight tonight. (Ha. Just kidding.)

Congrats on the loan, but more importantly – and even funnier – was that development on your editors. The embezzling, boozing skirt-chaser is now out? Enter Kelly the blue-haired, punk rock colleen. See? Life's a crapshoot, and your luck is already changing for the better. But color this east coast guy one dumb bunny. What the devil is Kokanee? A liquid form of cocaine? Except for prescriptions, I don't do drugs, but have hoisted a few frothy and bubbly liquids.

Lastly, on a more serious note, you asked about living in a maze. Don't we all? If not a maze, then it's a traveling circus. Or a bubble. On the inside looking out. Or on the outside looking in. There are days I swear we humans just can't win for trying. Nope, you ain't alone, young lady.

And good luck on that interview next week, Madam Mascara.

Peter – and the Wolf

(Was my middle name swiped from that Russian composer? I never thought to ask mom or dad.)

8.

Dear Happy Dancer,

It doesn't surprise me you aren't a smoker, because if you were I wouldn't be able to read you at all. Don't worry. I won't spread any rumours about you other than telling my English class that a New York writer is reviewing my manuscript. You say you aren't a writer, but from your emails I gather you are very adept at writing and vocally fluent when you want to be unlike those silent types with long hair who always look so sad and disillusioned. I think they're like that because of the amount of pot they smoke.

I encourage you to write because of your sense of humour and ability to spell, unlike my fellow classmates. Why don't you post something on Wordsmiths.net? A poem or story will do. I was soooo glad when other readers also commented on my work. I felt like I'd won an Academy Award. Well, almost!

Thirty isn't over the hill. If you live to a hundred you aren't even a third of the way there. I'm sure another gal will come along, but you need to open your mind to the possibility. Here's a hint. If a woman drops something, pick it up. They LOVE chivalry.

What kind of work do you do? Pilot? Race car driver? Veterinarian? If I look into my crystal ball, I figure you must have a job, but I keep seeing a desk.

Kokanee cocaine? LOL. Actually Kokanee is a cool, crisp, glacier beer brewed here in Creston, British Columbia. You must try it, but I guess it isn't sold in Manhattan. Come west, young man!

So my job interview went all right except for the fact I listed babysitting as my only paid job. I explained that I volunteer my time, cleaning and buying groceries for my parents and sister. In exchange, I have food and a roof over my head. The manager didn't say much, but kept looking at his watch. Finally, I asked him, "Do you need to be somewhere?" And he said, "Why? Do *you*?" So much for starting on good terms.

The manager called me yesterday to say, "Despite your lack of experience, you have some college education, so I've decided to hire you for a probationary period. I'll have Melanie train you to use the cash register. You will need a uniform, which we supply to new employees along with a 'Trainee' button. Since you will be working in cosmetics, you should come to work wearing make-up with your nails and hair looking impeccable. Please report for work on Saturday at 9 a.m."

I was pleased to get the job, but I knew he only hired me because of my dad. At least, I'll get paid more than minimum wage, and they give discounts to employees. I'll be stocking up on school supplies and candy.

I'm attaching my manuscript. THANK YOU SO MUCH! If you hate it, I can always work in cosmetics for the rest of my life. Ah, what a dreadful thought. I'm not sure about how it works in America, but don't worry about the copyright in Canada. Here it's copyrighted once it hits the page so to speak.

Ms. Mason emailed me that my article was accepted, but she had to shorten it to two hundred words and sent me the edit. I couldn't believe it, but she spelled my name wrong: Samantha Chew. What a dork!

Cheerio,
Writer in Training

9.

I immediately downloaded Sam's manuscript file to my flashdrive so I could enjoy reading some of it while having lunch at my desk. The bosses are adamant about us not having any personal items on their computers, so now I'd be able to plug it in whenever I wanted.

Resisting the impulse to dive in head first, I pondered an ironic fact: here I was, about to read her work – while she's been reading *me*.

Hmmm.

Exhibiting an unfamiliar quality of patience, a virtue I've never possessed, I waited until after my exquisite "dinner-*du-jour*" of yesterday's pepperoni pizza (cold) and coffee (steaming hot). Except for several minor errors of punctuation, spelling and grammar, the entire first half far exceeded my expectations generated by the original posted first chapter. It had far more in it than I'd anticipated: characters that I found myself deeply caring about and exotic, almost erotic, locales. Dialogue she'd devised rocketed off the page and crackled with unexpected surges of electricity, leaving only leftover whiffs of imaginary ozone within my mind, ears and soul.

Does Samantha realize what she *has* here? From the content of her e-mails, I doubt it.

Without wasting yet another New York minute, I wrote and finished the first installment of my critique, comments and deliberate low-key praise for her effort. I could not wait to attach it to the following e-mail:

Dear Trainee ~

Congrats on landing that job. (But only Saturdays?) Still, remember: "Bread helps; loot wins."

More kudos and props for the acceptance of your article, however heavily edited it was, but I laughed myself into a coma over the new editor's misspelling of your name. "Dork" is not the right term. Maybe the gal's still in the closet, but thinks of you as a potential chew-toy. (*Ouch*)

Thank you for attaching the manuscript of *The Boy Who Got Away*. I'm already halfway through those 212 pages. Funny – with your claiming to be psychic, did you know that 212 is a long-time Manhattan area code? I've been told it used to cover all of the five boroughs until the advent of fax machines and cell phones. Then, it seemed, every other block needed its own area code. 718. 347. 646. 917... But based on my unofficial comments in the attachment, you're hardly destined for a career as a "war paint" practitioner in the cosmetics section of Macy's or whatever upscale drugstore chain is popular in Vancouver these days.

Yeah, I do live in the big bad city and have been "writing" you these e-mail messages, so I guess it's not strictly a lie to be telling your pals that I'm a New York writer. (But it *is* a stretch, lady.) For the record, I do use Spellcheck more often than not. And whatever would I possibly post on the website? I am not the least bit creative. You said a poem. OK. Let me think of one here...

    10 Lines from a Lazy Poet

       1. ---------
       2. ---------
       3. ---------

Think it'll fly? No?

Me, neither.

Well, I'm not all that concerned about not having a steady g/f at the moment. Truth is I'm really not looking. Too damn busy with work. Friends of the opposite sex are always cool, but serious relationships can often take a serious toll. Been there, done that. I much prefer to hang out with or write to talented folks such as you. That's far more fun and entertaining in the long run. So, you see, Peter is *not* really such a wolf after all.

Untitled Story

Based on your advice, though, I did try to do the chivalrous thing on the subway last evening when a Puerto Rican gal dropped her keys to the floor of the car. As I bent down to pick them up, she blasted me: "They's mine's! Leave my chit alone, man!" (BTW, "man" is always pronounced "meng" in their very heavy Spanglish accent.) So much for chivalry in NYC, eh?

I realize it's none of my business, but do you have a b/f? If so, feel free to include stuff about him here, too. I don't mind.

You asked what kind of work I do. You were correct about the desk. While those Wall Street moneymakers are doing their business downtown, I work for a financial analysis firm located in midtown Manhattan. I majored in Business Administration while in college, with a minor in computer technology. Except for watching the rise and fall of Ponzi mastermind Bernie Madoff, who's now serving a one-hundred-fifty-year sentence in a Federal penitentiary, it's mind-numbing boredom, but that's the money-driven and digital world we all live in today. Gordon Gekko told us in the movie that "greed is good." There are days I think he might've been onto something, however abhorrent that concept may be to some.

I consider the pay decent, but a clerk down the hall recently posted a sign on her cubicle wall:

> *When I first started working, I used to dream of the day when I might be earning the salary I'm starving on now.*

Really, none of us have to walk around whining like city bureaucrats that they "get paid weekly – very *weakly*." NYC was rated last month in *am/NY*, one of our free daily newspapers, as the most expensive U.S. city in which to live, tied with Honolulu. Had I read that right – *Honolulu*? Hey, young lady, given a freakin' choice...

Thanks for that Kokanee clarification. I'd never heard of that brand of beer. Sounds pretty tasty. Tell you what. If I do a decent job of "reviewing" your prize novel, you can consider delivering me a six-pack, providing US customs will allow that. I mean, can you imagine the headlines? "Canadian Coed Beer Bootlegger Busted." We certainly wouldn't want that, would we? That would sure screw up the start of a beautiful friendship, to paraphrase Bogey's Rick character in *Casablanca*.

Now I think I'll go watch a DVD. Maybe one filmed up in Canada. Did you know there are more U.S. movies filmed there than in Hollyweird these days? True...because costs are so much lower.

Chock Full of ... Facts Peter

10.

Dear Pete the Lazy Poet,

You're kidding me you can't write. You are the king of one-liners. But I understand if you don't want to post your writing. If you aren't a writer, you don't have to deal with dorky editors or piles of rejection letters.

I'd say that working at a financial analysis firm isn't bad compared to my job at the cosmetics counter. On my first day, I knocked over a box of lipsticks and it took me half an hour to re-sort them. Then this woman came in, smelling like Chanel, wanting a complete makeover. I spent an hour with her, and she left without buying any make-up at all. Then Melanie told me that there is a thirty-dollar minimum purchase for customers who want their make-up done. How was I supposed to know?

My schedule is to work Wednesday nights and eight-hour shifts on Saturday and Sunday. I won't get rich, but I will get sore feet, wearing three-inch heels and standing all day.

In regards to expensive cities, Vancouver was listed as the second least affordable city in the world to live in after Hong Kong. I doubt I will ever be able to afford my own house in Vancouver unless I win the lottery or find a rich fellow.

You asked if I'm "attached." Let's just say I'm "detached" like the house I live in with my parents and sister. I met this guy Ronnie Petzler in the college cafeteria. He asked me if I had a pen. I said no and continued highlighting my reading notes. Then he said, "If not, can I offer you a ticket to the Canucks game tomorrow night?"

My ears were perked. "What's the catch?"

"No strings attached. Honestly."

We met the next day and he drove us down to the game. We had a couple of beers and joked around. When he dropped me home, he gave me a long kiss. For the next while, we talked on the phone and spent time together during breaks at school. He was sweet and affectionate and my attraction to him grew. I was taken aback when he said he was going to Montreal over spring break to see his old girlfriend.

"You never mentioned her before," I said.

"We have an open relationship," he said. "She dates women as well."

"Oh, you both like women?" I wasn't sure about dating him if he dated other people. I'd only known him for six weeks.

Before I could say anything else, he said, "I told her we're just friends. You're a pal." He punched me in the shoulder.

So here I was infatuated with this fellow and, to him, I was nothing more than a pal. So after spring break, I saw him talking to another girl on a bench at college. He had his arm around her and brushed her hair with his hand. I walked right by and didn't say a word. So as that so-called relationship is in demise, I'm flying solo.

In regards to *Boys Who Got Away* in my real life, Ron is No. 5. I've had four other failed relationships (if you can call a date a relationship) including a boy who asked me out to a dance. I refused to slow dance with him because he was shorter than me and his eyes were the exact height of my developing breasts. I was a self-conscious adolescent.

Let me know what you think of the manuscript. I hope you have good things to say about it; otherwise I'll be applying for dead-end jobs until the cows come home. If I can ever afford a flight to New York, I'll let you know and I'll bring the beer!

Looking for answers,
Chewy

11.

Hey, Chewbacca, time to let down your hair (like Rapunzel), unwind and relax.

I was surprised at the treatment by ex-Ron – which sounds like two of our corrupt corporations: Exxon and Enron. Don't know you in person, but I think you deserve a whole lot better from the opposite gender. And regarding his other gal pal who likes women, here's a good story I recall...

One night at a 2nd Avenue singles bar, a guy fast approaching a condition known as being "three sheets to the wind" was boasting that he and his lesbian buddies were super tight. He'd screamed out, "I *love* lesbians!" When someone stupid enough asked him why, he informed us all proudly and loudly, "Hell, they like a lot of the same stuff I do..."

Anyhow, since you've recently become a pal of mine, I promise not to punch you in the arm – or shoulder. Ever. End of pep talk.

I'm glad that you have more hours for that cosmetics job than just Saturdays, but hey, everyone makes mistakes when they start. Do they really expect you to walk on water? End of sermon. (This from a non-church-going kinda guy, a place I avoid religiously.)

Me, a king of one-liners? Hardly. Probably stole 'em from some late-night TV show comedian. I have a really good memory, just like a sponge. Sometimes it's frightening. Anyway, in entering this guilty plea, I would like to remind the court that I once had a high school g/f named Cleo – and known by everyone, friends and frenemies alike, as the "Queen of Denial." End of case.

You mentioned hockey. It reminded me of an urban legend about a street hockey player in the Bronx. It's said that the guy had caught a puck in his mouth, but everyone in his neighborhood thought it was just a case of bad gums. End of old jokes.

I never got interested in sports. Mainly because I was so bad at them. Even Dodgeball in school – America's perverse twist on stoning. Here's a quickie rundown of how I look at most sports:

Football: Refrigerators on steroids
Baseball: Perpetual little boys hitting and chasing a little white ball
Golf: Ditto the above except most are old fat men
Tennis: Ditto the above for both sweaty sexes, but the little balls are green
Basketball: For pituitary freaks hanging from basket hoops
Bowling: Tenpins for drunks with no talents except heaving their 16-lb. balls around
Cycling: Speedy racers in aerodynamically designed rubber pants
Racing: Speedy drivers with suicidal urges
Skiing: Speedy downhill racers with suicidal urges
Hockey: Speedy skaters in masks with suicidal urges
Soccer: "Look, ma, no hands! Look, ma, more concussions!"
Boxing: Prehistoric purveyors of barbarism
Wrestling: Overweight bozos who flunked acting classes
Synchronized Swimming: If one drowns, does the other have to drown, too?

The movie I watched the other night was *KAW* (2007), filmed in Canada. It was similar in a way to Alfred Hitchcock's *The Birds*, a classic from 1963. Did you ever see that one on TV? If you did, then you might be surprised to learn that actor Rod Taylor, Hitchcock's lead, was also given a good part in this one, only as a much older guy. Natch, but still a neat homage.

Because *KAW* was only about ninety minutes, I squeezed in another flick, one a bit shorter, *The Moth Diaries* (2011), also from Canada – and Ireland. It was an official selection in the Toronto International Film Festival. The Venice Film Festival, too. Life at Brangwyn, a prestigious but strict private prep school, was like living in a gulag, yet the girls always found some way to party or to be with boys – just before things got real weird. I liked Valerie Tian a lot. She played Charlie, a Chinese rebel who got expelled halfway through for tossing a chair through an upstairs window while on drugs. (She – not the window or chair – was high.)

Untitled Story

On the IMDb website, I learned that Valerie lives in your neck of the woods. She's a cutie. Do you happen to know her? You're both about the same age. For all I know, you two might be good friends. If so, can you introduce me? Pretty please?

The downside was that I overslept and reported to work an hour late. Caught holy hell from you-know-who. So I had to stay an hour longer to make it up. That's why this e-mail is being written later than usual. Maybe I should buy a louder alarm clock or set the radio to a heavy metal station.

The weekend will be here again soon. Time for me to rest up and lick my wounds. Have a good one yourself. Party till it's 1999, they like to sing. Catch ya next week...

Pete (about to party, too? Nah.)

12.

Dear Film Buff,

I get the sense you are a fan of movies. Did you catch the Oscars recently? Ellen DeGeneres was hilarious as the Master of Ceremonies, passing out lotto scratch cards to people who were nominated, but didn't win, and pizza deliveries to those in the front row. She took a photo of a group including herself and posted it on Twitter. It went viral and crashed Twitter.

One thing about working in cosmetics is you don't meet many male customers. Not that I mind. I did aid one fellow looking for perfume for his girlfriend. Perfume is hard to buy because the scents smell different on different people. A lot of people don't like scents nowadays on the account of adverse reactions. I think a bar of soap does the trick for most.

Kreative Kelly, the new school paper editor, accepted my article for publication. If she gets my name wrong in print, I'm going to raise hell. As for your Chewbacca reference, and as far as *Star Wars* goes, I identify much more with Princess Leia for obvious reasons. I don't wear my hair in buns over my ears, but she holds her own in battling with the dark side.

If Ron were a *Star Wars* character, he'd be one of the aliens at the bar, an opportunist looking to get drunk, making underhanded deals, and seeking alien women. I hope his spaceship explodes. I hate him since he left me a phone message saying, "Sorry, Sam, but I have to break it off. It isn't fun anymore." Shit! I didn't even have the pleasure of breaking it off myself or a chance to say what I thought of him.

Looking for No. 6,
Princess Sam

I wondered if he's finished reading my manuscript, but was a little unsure about asking him what he thought of the conclusion. I decided to be patient. Wait and see. It was interesting that I could connect with Pete even though we lived thousands of miles apart.

Ah, the wonders of the Internet. He was his own person, with no apologies, but I sensed he fought within himself on occasion.

I turned off my laptop and got into bed, falling asleep dreaming of winning an Oscar for writing a screenplay, tripping on stage and landing in the arms of George Clooney.

I dig older men.

13.

I can blame only myself. One, for not replying fast enough to Samantha's latest e-mail, and two, for purchases of items I was magnetically drawn to, almost against my will. What has sent me spiraling into confusion, then a deep depression and, ultimately, into total inaction, were those damnable DVDs.

I'd purchased a movie for less than ten dollars at one of the video shops along 14th Street near Union Square and got to watch it that evening. *Passengers* was a 2008 film directed by Rodrigo Garcia, someone totally unfamiliar to me. As I learned in the bonus features, it was shot in Vancouver. Seemingly about survivors of a plane crash on the beach of the Spanish Banks, its finale took a paranormal twist that I wasn't expecting. Not at all. That ending of crossing the line between this world and the next shook me up and rattled around inside my brain for several days.

The effect was compounded that weekend at a Saturday yard sale I attended in Brooklyn. There was a shoebox of blank and used cassette tapes I felt I could somehow use, so I bought them for a paltry two bucks. When I returned to my flat, I played one that sported a handwritten label. Contained on one special twelve-minute tape were a few professionally produced jingles. There was a standard 30-second offering, followed by a catchy Christmas variation for the same outfit. Would anyone believe they were for a shopping mall in Vancouver?

Hell, *I* couldn't believe it.

The California advertising agency which created them had added a 1974 date at the bottom of the label, a full decade before I made my worldly debut in the Brooklyn section of Planet Earth. Does Vancouver Mall even exist now in 2014? I must remember to ask Samantha eventually.

On Sunday I traveled to an uptown Manhattan street fair where I bought a book of poems by an obscure writer who, in all likelihood, published it himself way back in the '60s. The Hippie Era. On the subway ride home later, I thought I'd pass out cold when one of the poems turned out to be an ethereal mood piece set on the Lion's Gate Bridge – in Vancouver.

Have I morphed into a human divining rod for all things Vancouver? I was forced to ask myself over and over, "What the hell gives here?"

But it didn't end there.

On Monday, at Academy Records on W. 18th Street, a used DVD with a cover printed sideways attracted my attention. T.F. Mou was listed as the 1995 director for *Black Sun: The Nanking Massacre*. From a high school world history class, I recalled that this incident had occurred during the time when Japan attacked China prior to the official outbreak of World War II in 1939. This had been two years earlier. I have no interest in events from almost eighty years ago, but this 95-minute documentary selling for all of $8.99 would not allow me to replace it in the bin. It failed to release the grasp my right hand had on it, and the left was already reaching into my back pocket for my wallet.

I questioned my purchase all the way home. Was it an impulse buy?

I was left with no satisfactory answer.

Wednesday was the capper. I don't much care for the current trend of American horror and splatter movies. They are as much a complete turn-off as those mindless, repetitive porno flicks. The Japanese, however, find psychological fear from within, and I find that a refreshing change-of-pace for an overworked genre. J&R Music near City Hall had a hot 50% discount sale going on for its ever-dwindling stock of DVDs, and I was fast to snatch the only copy of a Takashi Shimizu film from 2005. I'd liked his *Ju-On* and *The Grudge* series previously, so why not *Reincarnation*?

I soon found that I was as drawn into his film as I'd been with Samantha's first chapter, which is also when some of this weird stuff seemed to begin, but at a much lower level. Almost subconsciously. My mind is still reeling as I try to recount specific events within the story and the complex feelings they produced in me. Shimizu's talented, youthful and highly professional cast and crew had left me devastated long after the closing credits.

Work has become impossible, and I called in sick three days straight. I made no calls, not even to the doctor from my health plan. I failed – no, refused – to answer my phones whenever they rang or vibrated. I even turned off my voicemail. No interest left in conversing while the wild thoughts danced around inside my brain.

God, if I don't snap out of this – like, real soon – I'm afraid I may have to ask for that prickly bastard of a boss for an extended leave of absence.

The worst part? I fear my recent non-contact with Samantha will cause her to worry, even though I'm probably nothing more to her than a quirky pen pal who entertains her long-distance.

But if I do resume the friendship, I think it might be a very wise move to give her my cell, home landline and work numbers.

The last one, that is, provided I still have a job...

14.

I was perplexed. I had sent an email to Pete two weeks ago and he hadn't written back. I tried to tell myself perhaps he was busy or maybe his computer crashed, but was there something I had written that ticked him off?

For the life of me, I didn't know what his reason was. Maybe he'd lost interest because, face it, I wasn't that interesting. Did I bore him with my stories? Perhaps he has found a new girlfriend or got hit by a car and was undergoing surgery to fix his broken bones or was he sentenced to life in a wheelchair because he couldn't walk anymore? He was probably too young for a stroke or heart attack, but couldn't you get cancer at any age? Hmmm. What to do?

I plugged in my email password and composed something new.

Dear Silent Stranger,

I hadn't heard from you in two weeks, not that I'm counting. Are you okay? Or did you lose your two typing fingers? If you did, check the Lost and Found. (I don't mean to be sassy, just joking.)

Did you not like the ending to my manuscript?

Are you on vacation, or did something happen at work?

If you don't want to write me anymore, I'll be sad for a few days and shed a tear, but I'll get over it. Life goes on, right?

Worry Wart,
Sam as always

I pressed SEND. I knew not to put "all my eggs in one basket," but I didn't have another friend like him. And I'd much rather invest time into getting to know Pete than meeting certain college students who were more into alcohol and partying than having an intelligent conversation. Sure, I liked social drinking, but not to the point of stupor and loss of consciousness.

Pete might get back to me or not. Did he judge me for

something I said, I didn't know. Despite my sixth sense, I didn't always make good choices. Even if one's logic says no, one will make risky decisions based on emotion, fear or temptation.

Was I a schmuck for sharing my personal failures and disappointments with someone I'd never seen?

15.

Subject: I ESCAPED – DO NOT PAY RANSOM!

Hey, Princess Sam ~

Your pal, the "Silent Stranger," has returned to the Land of the Living after a brief setback. I apologize for that silly header above, but I only wanted to emulate your earlier humor – and to let you know I still have mine, mostly intact. I'm sorry even more that I may have caused undue concern on your part, so allow me to try to remedy some of that. For now, I just needed you to know that I wasn't arrested for passing bogus Ben Franklins or hospitalized with scurvy and rickets or threatened with deportation because Vladimir Putin was showing much too much military muscle in Ukraine and Crimea. As for the real story of what I went through, you'll learn more later, but in dribs and drabs, when I feel up to it. I hope you'll understand better then...

Until then, dash all those thoughts of heresy, pilgrim. My never writing to you again? Still, I was pissed off at Ronnie Rambo's actions and frost-cold insensitivity. You – not any fun? Sorry that cretins like him give decent guys a black eye. May his next conquest bestow on him a serious case of the crabs.

You will find five attachments – 3 are text, 2 are jpegs:

Attachment 1: To me, the *most* important. You'll find three phone numbers should you ever need to contact me – cell, landline at home and work. I don't expect you to pay for long-distance calls, so if reverse charges are allowed from your end in Canada, I don't mind paying for them. You've become too dear a friend during the past month or two that I don't want to lose that. 'Nuff said.

Attachment 2: I LUVED your novel. Here's my complete critique. What more can I say except that this work of yours needs to see the light of day for many a future reader? And f-a-s-t.

Attachment 3: There are ten pages of suggestions, spelling fixes, typo corrections, etc. Go back into your manuscript to make this as perfect as possible. Why? Well, among my company's clients are several people from the publishing world, and I know them well. Later, we'll see if any of these fish take the bait. As long as it's your own work, which I'm sure it is (plagiarism will only get you jail time and heavy-duty monetary fines), and if you are willing to escape from the Curse of Panda Eyes at the cosmetics counter, just give me a green light.

Attachment 4 (Jpeg 1): Just so you don't envision me as a freak of nature, here's a recent pic of the Menace of Moscow.

Attachment 5 (Jpeg 2): One of "Damn" and me from two years ago. Yeah, you'll spot a little family resemblance, but *blond* hair? God forgive me, but sometimes I wonder if mama wasn't spending too much quality time with that Polish milkman nine months before he showed up.

Now, on to some things you'd brought up, like the Academy Awards on Sunday, March 2. I did watch them with the multi-costumed host whose style and humor I loved. The pizza bit really cracked me up, and I laughed even harder when she pocketed the audience guy's twenty bucks all for herself. Ended up guessing a dozen winners correctly and, despite the landslide for *Gravity*, I applauded like a possessed wild man as Lupita Nyong'o won for Best Supporting Actress and *12 Years a Slave* for Best Picture.

On the downside, the "In Memoriam" section showed names and photos of several people whose work I've loved and respected, but didn't know they had passed on. One was Ray Harryhausen, the stop-action Dynamation expert whose sci-fi epics (*Beast from 20,000 Fathoms*, *It Came from Beneath the Sea* and *Earth vs. the Flying Saucers*), plus his *Jason and the Argonauts* and Sinbad adventure films thrilled many generations of kids, including my dad; another was author Elmore Leonard whose current hit series, "Justified" (now in its fifth season), has me hooked; and then there was Richard Matheson (*I Am Legend* and *The Incredible Shrinking Man*, "Twilight Zone" episodes and far too many short stories for me to name here). They, and others such as Shirley Temple and Philip Seymour Hoffman, will sorely be missed.

You'd signed off one of your e-mails as "Chewy." Han Solo called his Wookie pal "Chewie," so I just picked up on that, but never meant to imply that you're huge or a growler covered with hair. Yep. Princess Sam fits you world's better. And those buns of hers? Buns of steel, eh? LOL. (As for Ronnie Rambo, he should be a future headliner in *Star Warts*. For better context, please feel free to refer to my crabs comment above.)

Listen, after my still unexplained lengthy absence from your inbox, I can't ask you for a speedy reply, but if you choose to, it will do a world of good for my spirits. Many thx in advance.

Pop-Up Peter (but feeling more like a Whack-A-Mole these days)

16.

I was pleased as punch that not only did Mr. Petrovich like my novel, but he also knew publishers! I was so excited to tell my sister Allie that I tripped over a lamp and broke a vase. It was an ugly vase, but my mother noticed right away and took away my first paycheck as punishment. She told me to sign it over and she'd deposit it into her savings account. So much for buying a new pair of shoes or glitter for my nails.

I went through Pete's corrections and edits and howled at his funny comments as well. He was as entertaining as any movie I'd ever seen.

The Menace of Moscow turned out to be a good-looking fellow. I knew he was thirty, but appeared younger than that—a baby-faced Russian-American. Did he have money? Why was he single? I wanted to know. He didn't look the least bit like the Wall Street type in a leather jacket and cool shades. A rebel without a cause was more like it.

Eagerly, I composed a new email.

Dear James Dean,

Thanks for sending your photo – twice. You look more like James Dean than a financial wizard if you know what I mean. Are you sure you aren't in the wrong line of work? Hollywood is calling you to play either James Bond or Jason Bourne. I am surprised the ladies aren't lining up for tickets to spend long evenings with you on the couch, watching a rather large collection of DVDs which I get a sense of the ones you own.

Seriously, why aren't you married? They say all the good ones are already taken. What's your story? Ingrown toenails or an addiction to Japadogs? (Not that there's anything wrong with Japadogs, but too much of anything can be bad for you.) I mean, what's wrong with the women in your life that you aren't settled down with a blonde babe, a mortgage and a kid on the way?

I'm a little shy to actually contact you by phone unless it's an emergency. So I added your phone numbers on speed dial just under 9-1-1. I'm attaching my phone numbers, too, but I warn you my mother will hear any messages you leave on our house line. She's curious about you because I told her I had a pen pal in New York. She said, "Is he gay or a crook? Because you always seem to attract the wrong type."

It's nice to have family support.

Yesterday I thought I'd died and gone to heaven. But it was a mistake and I'm still here. God bless cosmeticians everywhere. We make women feel more beautiful while generating revenue for drugstores around the world. I'm starting to dream about false eyelashes stuck to my eyes and cosmetic bags that double as wallets to avoid pickpockets. Great idea, huh?

Billy Jean

17.

I felt progressively better throughout the week and decided to send Samantha a brief note late on Wednesday evening. This much longer attachment contained an explanation of my two-week-long offline "disappearance" that I hoped she would believe. Rather than provide a blow-by-blow description of my mini-meltdown, I downplayed it by writing it off as a minor panic attack which had occurred during a routine business conference call. Just something out of the ordinary and only somewhat disconcerting. Nothing more.

"It happens all the time to others," I wrote, citing the case of a national television news reporter who'd experienced one on-the-air several years before. I also made light of all those Vancouver coincidences, but withheld my reaction brought on by the Nanking documentary and Shimizu's mind-bending film. That would remain my secret, at least until I knew her somewhat better. My sole reason: I'm not a certifiable whack job, so why spook the kid?

Friday at work, by custom, was Casual Day. Lucy had all the guys sucking in their stomachs as she strolled in and strutted about the office. She paraded around in a pair of jeans that could've been sprayed-on at home earlier that morning. In the crowded elevator on the way to lunch, I overheard Mr. Gino, a new office manager, casually whisper to Salvatore Ferro, another boss, "If she coulda squeezed a quarter into her back pocket, we woulda all known for sure if it was heads or tails."

"Yeah," Sal said in his usual loud voice, "hers is certainly one world-class ass."

His comment and their constant childish snickering turned a few frowning female heads, and I was barely able to stifle a guffaw at the boss's sexist but highly accurate comeback line. It also made me recall something else Lucy had done recently that had driven all the guys into a lecherous frenzy. While reviewing documents at her desk, she slowly devoured a Tootsie Roll lollipop just like a human suction pump. When word got around, male workers found any and all reasons to pass her desk. Others watched from a distance as they let their imaginations run wild, and all the while emitting occasional low-level moans. And at no time did the eyes of this seemingly innocent woman ever look up from her work or otherwise acknowledge the erotic effects of her actions.

The remainder of this workday was as boring as any other day. Shortly after five, I wrapped up a few last-minute details on one project and, calling it a day, I thought it best to use the facilities before the crowded subway ride home and headed down the hall to the men's room. I grinned as I remembered some jokester's spin on Einstein's Theory of Relativity – the relative length of a minute depends on which side of the bathroom door you're on. Isn't that the truth?

As I washed up, I thought of a variation on old soda ad: Never let 'em tell ya Pepsi is the only pause that refreshes. With the hand dryer roaring at full blast on the far wall by the window, I failed to hear the restroom door open and close. Then I felt a pair of arms and hands encircling my chest and waist from behind. Feminine arms and hands.

"What the hell?" I turned to face a smirking Lucy. "Hey, what are you *doing*? If anyone walks in and catches you here, you're as good as fired, Lucy. You'd be instant toast."

She threw her head back and laughed. "Everybody go home already."

"Yeah? I'm thinking maybe you've watched that nightclub toilet scene in *Scarface* one time too many."

She playfully pushed me against the wall and moved in closer, her left leg between mine and her right hand slowly but steadily moving south of my beltline. She said with a pout, "Aw, bay-bee, I been watchin' you all week long. You be too uptight. No good."

As her hand found the object of her intended search, she gave it a gentle squeeze with her fingers while placing a small piece of paper in my shirt pocket with her free hand.

"What's that?" My voice sounded shallow and hollow.

"Where I live. For you to come over later. Nine o'clock? I de-stress you. I real good."

I turned my head away before she made more of an attempt to move in closer and insert the tip of her tongue into my ear. I searched for something to say to change her one-track mind.

"I wouldn't count on it, Lucy."

She made a disapproving face. "Don' tell me you a *maricon*? No, not *you*."

"In your dreams. Straight arrow all the way. It's just that you're just not my type."

Her mouth generated a wicked smile as her dark, devil's eyes bored like twin jackhammers into mine. "Oh? What ees your type? Tell Lucy. I be whatever you want."

"Asian. I like Asian gals." Words poured out of my mouth in rapid-fire succession. "They really, really turn me on. You have no idea..."

She waved her other hand to dismiss my claim. "No beeg deal. I send out for chop suey an' rice an' soy sauce. All the slimy stuff. I tape my eyes to make 'em slanty. Then we get it on hot an' heavy, yes?"

"No," I said, pushing her away from me. "Go home, lady. Take a cold shower. But I ain't your man. Not tonight. Not any night."

Lucy mumbled something nasty which could've been a curse in her native tongue, but I couldn't have cared less. What I wanted at the moment was to get the hell out of there – and fast. I barreled through the men's room door and shot an over-the shoulder glance behind me. She did not appear to be following through the now-deserted office. I made a bee-line for the elevator and entered it alone, very glad of that. The ride was swift, and the ground floor never looked so good to me.

On the homeward bound commute, I reviewed the sequence of events while trying to determine her approximate age. In her late thirties? Mid-forties? Age-wise, Lucy was a difficult read, but the undercurrent of her raw passion ran deep. I dug out the white slip of paper she'd slipped into my pocket and read it. Her address was up in Spanish Harlem – a no man's land for a lily-white guy like me. Besides, that woman made me feel sleazy. How many showers would it take for me to feel clean again?

I crumpled the paper in disgust and tossed it onto the already-filthy platform when the train car's doors opened at the next station.

Then I questioned why I'd blurted out that bullshit about Asian women turning me on? Jeez, I'd never dated one in my life, and the only one I've ever corresponded with is a Canadian college kid a continent away. Besides, I don't even know what the hell she looks like.

Ah, Samantha, have you been casting psychic, mystical spells over the Internet to play around with my confused head? What the hell is *really* going on with me? And how will I ever deal with that horny, hot tamale of a Mexican come Monday morning? Upon further reflection, it might be a good idea to relieve myself at the Starbuck's down the block for the next few days...

* * *

I hoped this weekend would be restful and pleasantly uneventful. I wasn't that lonesome or anywhere near desperate enough to be having a one-night stand – or any other type of an extended affair – especially with a pig wearing hot pink lipstick.

On a late Saturday morning, I finished the upcoming week's food shopping, cramming an armful of frozen dinners and half-gallon tubs of ice cream into my freezer. Later I walked over to several neighborhood bookshops just to browse through the aisles, but I saw nothing to interest me and didn't lay out as much as a single dime.

I spent Sunday bicycling around Central Park with its trees and flowers in bloom after the past harsh winter we'd endured. Yet all afternoon, while avoiding dogs and small children – all on leashes – plus frisky and sometimes aggressive squirrels darting in front of me, my mind kept getting sidetracked with thoughts of my little buddy, the authoress/sorceress. I found myself wondering what antics or misadventures she might be experiencing at that very moment at a drugstore in some Vancouver shopping mall.

Sweating and dreading work as I arrived to clock in early Monday morning, I couldn't help but notice that Lusty Lucy, now wearing a plain, respectable, knee-length dress, had never once attempted to make eye contact with me. The woman ignored me all day as if I were the original Invisible Man himself.

Thank you, Lord. An answer to a poor guy's humble prayer.

18.

I spent Friday morning listening to a lecture on the mating habits of apes in anthropology class. I doodled on my notepad only to realize I had scribbled Peter three times with a heart around it. Ah, dammit. I was falling for someone who lived thousands of miles away and who probably thought I was wet behind the ears.

He was probably a financial wizard with a portfolio of stocks and bonds and looking for someone much more sophisticated than a college sophomore. I ached for a backrub to relax the tension in my neck and shoulders. Finally, the bell rang. I grabbed my notepad and moved toward the door.

"Samantha, may I have a word with you?" The professor took off his glasses and gestured for me to stay behind.

The classroom emptied out until he and I were the only ones left.

"Yes, Mr. Johnson?" I looked at him earnestly, hoping he hadn't noticed I dozed off for ten minutes during his slide show.

"You are a good student?"

"Ah, I guess. I have a 3.8 grade point average."

"Would you be able to take on some duties for me? I think it would benefit both of us. I need a marker for my first year class."

"Is that allowed? I mean, am I qualified?"

"Of course. And I can pay you."

"Oh, in that case, I could spare four or five hours a week."

"Okay. I'd rather you didn't spread it around that you are now my teaching assistant. You know how gossip is."

I nodded.

He put out his hand and gave mine a squeeze. "Good. Can you come to my office now?" I nodded again and accompanied him down the elevator to the basement. He unlocked the door to a small, cluttered office. "Take a seat and I'll get the tests and answer key." He fumbled through his files on the desk and put a stack of paper in front of me as I sat on a chair in desperate need of reupholstering. "Here you go."

Then he did something I wasn't prepared for. Standing behind me, he squeezed my shoulders gently and ran his fingers along the nape of my neck. "You seem a little tense, Sam." He began to knead my back with his hands.

I responded by closing my eyes as I felt his gentle caresses easing my tight muscles. I didn't really think about the backrub being inappropriate, but rather as a rather pleasing experience. He whispered in my ear, "You're beautiful, Sam. Your skin is so smooth." Then his lips pressed against my neck.

What the hell was that? Completely caught off guard, I almost fell off my chair.

"Just relax."

"Aren't we here to look at the exams?" I avoided his gaze.

"Shall we take a look?" He brushed against me to pick up the file. I could smell his cologne.

I hesitated. I thought if I made a fuss about the kiss, he would ridicule me or knock me down a grade. If I reported him, it was his word against mine and he really hadn't done anything illegal. I was flattered he came on to me, and a kiss was harmless, right? He ended my pondering before I could sort through my feelings.

"We're adults here. I could help you through school. Give you a reference to any university you want or aid with a scholarship application. All I ask is that we –"

Before he could finish the sentence, someone knocked on the door. The door scraped open and a woman leaned into the cramped office. "Dick, we have a staff meeting."

"Oh, yes. I'll be there in a moment," Mr. Johnson said. "Sorry, Sam. We'll continue this conversation later."

"Well, I'll be going," I said. Without taking the file, I maneuvered around Mr. Johnson and the woman and slid out the door. He called after me, but I kept walking.

Sometimes you need to get out of a situation before it moves into unknown territory. He didn't invite me back to his office again. I guess he found someone else to mark exams. Afterwards, I felt that I had been skittish to leave. He wasn't that unattractive and he could have helped me. Regrets are funny that way. Did I lose out or prevent a problem?

Working in cosmetics didn't seem so bad after all. At least I had a job if my professor gave me a "B" because I wouldn't play ball. What a dick, that Dick.

19.

     Samantha's last e-mail was sitting there for two days without a reply. Time for me to get the lead out of my pants, as Papa Boris always used to tell me when I wasn't fast enough to suit him.

Subject: I SNORE. THAT'S WHY.

To "Billy Jean" from "James Dean" (LMAO) ~

Were you referencing a huge #1 Jacko hit song from the year I was born? If so, *tres* cool. ;)

And how did you know we had a Japadog restaurant in NYC? It was located over on St. Mark's Place in the East Village, but the place was boarded up when I passed by in April. Too many good companies are going under lately. I'd be willing to bet American dollars to Dunkin' Donuts you'll be telling me next that some displaced Japanese folks up Vancouver way were responsible for starting a chain of them there.

Yeah, some have told me my snoring sounded far worse than any loggers with buzz saws up in the Pacific Northwest. Nowadays pharmacies have adhesive gadgets like tiny band-aids to place on the bridge of the nose at bedtime. I'd bought a box, but since I'm not keeping ravishing fashion models awake nights – and for all the other wrong reasons – the box stays mostly in a drawer.

Your mom's questions and comments cracked me up big time, but I'll bet she's a real sweetie.

As for your questions, seriously, I've never been fortunate in meeting Miss Right. You'd think that living here in the most populated city in the country would bring a female bonanza for any available guy. Not true. And just as well. Many guys here are total jerks. Lost causes. Some ladies, too. Recently, I had to fight off an oversexed dame in my office. She gave up in disgust, figuring I was one of the Village People skipping and holding hands with the boys. Not true, either. The point is that I like to be able to pick and choose, but there's no rush. If Cupid should decide to shoot an arrow into any available (and exposed) part of my anatomy, then I'll go wild soon enough over that "Special Someone." Until that happens, it's just a waiting game. And a very patient one.

Don't ever feel shy about calling me collect in the future if you deem it important. And thanks for providing your home number. The reason I never asked for it is because it seemed too nosy on my part. Too intrusive. You have a right to your privacy, and I won't overstep that boundary. So have no fear about your mom's eavesdropping on messages that I haven't left.

Now, for the next step on your book. I trust you've made whatever file fixes were necessary. Good. If you are serious about bypassing the usual mailbox-clogging route of rejection slips and using me instead as a "go-between," I can present it to several people I know once I have your official green light and a final edit in hand. One middle-aged fellow is a book editor for a known publisher. Same for a lady, but with a rival company. She's brassy, sassy and all the rest of that jazz, but as sharp as the proverbial tack – or a rose bush thorn. One other gent is also an associate editor, and the last is a successful woman agent who has represented many authors you likely know or have read. She's got a great sense of humor, too.

I'm willing to approach these people, off-the-record and one at a time, because I'm ecstatic about *The Boy Who Got Away*. You've captured something universal. Easy for writers to say; very hard to achieve. Ask any and all of those authors who wallpaper their apartments with the abundance of aforementioned rejection slips.

But this is important for you to know: I want nothing from you in return. Nada. Zilch. El zippo. No money. No percentage of sales. No gratuitous sex. Not even the 6-pack of Kokanee we kidded about. No hidden agendas, as they call 'em. *Nyet*.

So, what's in it for me, you ask? Being a part of helping to make it available to others is a reward in itself. Besides, Mama Larisa always told me when I was little, "Petya, my son, if you do good for peoples, it becomes even better thing in eyes of God. Always remember."

And I have.

Do-Gooder Pete

P.S.: On second thought, kiddo, I might accept a grateful hug.

    I paused my index finger for many a long moment above the command to send. Was I truthful with Sam? Completely honest? Did I want nothing from her besides her friendship – and a hug?
    Yeah, I guess...

20.

Dear Pete,

    I was on the verge of a meltdown when I received your email, which turned my week around. The meltdown was caused by my goldfish passing away. I woke up and there he was, floating motionless in the tank. We had a small ceremony in memory of the little guy, and my sister flushed him down the toilet. My mom said I can get a new one, but I felt I needed to mourn his demise as he journeys to goldfish heaven. We have two remaining pets, a Scottish Terrier and a parakeet. Fingers crossed they're okay without their little buddy.

    I dried my tears and focused on your message. I'm ecstatic you'd consider helping me find a publisher for my novel! There are benevolent beings on earth, and you are truly one of them. Forgive me if I don't call you a Good Samaritan, but rather a captain of a ship in a stormy sea, rescuing the fair maiden from a lifeboat of anonymity. Thank you from the bottom of my novice heart. Even if they say no, at least I tried, and I'll go out in a blaze of glory as the girl who wrote the book that got away!

    As requested, I'm sending my revised manuscript, synopsis and short bio so you have it. I don't really have writing credits other than the piece in the school paper. But I can spell if that's of any value.

    No gratuitous sex, beer or money as payment? I can live with that, but a good deed has a way of coming back to you. It's true. I found a quarter on the drugstore floor and gave it back to an elderly woman who was looking in her purse. She was so grateful that she put in a good word for me with the manager at the checkout line.

    As a parallel to events in your life, I too was accosted, not by a co-worker, but my anthropology professor, Dick Johnson. He kissed me! Was I being a prude to not accept his advances? What is with people? Aren't students off limits? I am over eighteen so maybe he thought it was okay. Tell me, was the office tigress who pounced on you in heat? Biologically speaking, it is possible she was hormonal or on the rebound. Office sex and politics don't mix, so wise choice on your part to fend her off. However, unwanted advances can be difficult to handle because sometimes you wonder if you made the right decision. What would have happened if you did go down that road? Relationships aren't forever anyway. What's wrong with a little fun? As for your Miss Right, she's probably dating my Mr. Right right now.

Sometimes even if you think you found the right person, they slip through your fingers or worse, they reveal their ugly habits after the ceremony like laziness or chalking up expenses on their credit cards that they can't pay off.

For you, snoring isn't a relationship-breaker – or is it? Unless you are breaking windows because of loud vibrations, can't a woman in love invest in earplugs?

In the meantime, I'm sticking to school and work. I'm also considering going to Animals Anonymous where people talk about pet problems. I'm kidding. Goldie is a goner. No coming back from a watery grave. No reincarnation. ("Goldie" is a strange name for a male fish, but we didn't know he was male when we named him.)

Please let me know what the publishers have to say. I hear sometimes it takes months for them to respond, if at all. As it goes in the world of writing.

Signing off with a virtual hug,
Sam

21.

Wowie kazowie, Samantha's really gonna brain me for this opener...

Subject: Goldie Loss

Although I felt for you, I hesitate to mention my fave snacks are Goldfish. (They are the cheese crackers made by Pepperidge Farms locally, so please don't report me to the Humane Society.) And we had a cat once named "Ben Hur." At first we'd just called it Ben – until it had kittens.

I reviewed the manuscript with corrections. It looks great. And you're welcome for whatever results are the byproduct of my feeble efforts. I'll have the synopsis ready for the first of those four who stops by the office beginning next week. As I get feedback, so will you. I promise.

Re your recent Close Encounter of the Predator Kind? I winced. A kiss isn't the worst thing that could've happened, but it *was* totally inappropriate. How old is Mr. Johnson, anyway? I howled when you wrote his first name was Dick. He certainly lives up to his name. Isn't the dude getting enough at home if he's married? I cannot tolerate any sophisticated male professors who violate the rights of students they are sworn to educate. Same with local cops here. Supposed to protect us, there are some who have made the local news (and were later fired) for robbing teens, minorities or foreigners they can't stomach. You're right not to report him because no one will believe you, but keep your ears and eyes open. If he made a pass at you, undoubtedly there will be others he's hit on. Always remember there's strength in numbers.

As for my office incident, her name is Lucy – and always in heat. There's something about her that repels rather than attracts me. She hasn't spoken to me since, so I figure she now has a steady shmoo to roll in the clover with. If not, maybe I'll leave a wrapped sex toy in her desk drawer on her day off. Ha.

By the way, just so you know, I'm no Sunday school puritan. If two consenting adults want to entertain each other, I'm down with that. Perfectly normal. As for my snoring? How about I make a tape and mail it? You can be the judge as to whether you'd endure it or invest in ear plugs...

No, NO, Sam. Ignore the last suggestion. It came out all wrong. I wasn't implying or suggesting anything of the sort – and I don't plan to be teaching at your college, either. Ay. Color me red...

Ironic that you mentioned reincarnation. Because we know each other a bit better at this point, I owe you a more in-depth reason for what had transpired a while back when I went offline. Off-kilter was more like it, but I'll need to take a long running start before jumping headlong into it.

Do you know what it means when people "associate" or "disassociate" with books or movies? It means they're fully into it or not at all, just something to pass the time without any emotional investment. Since childhood, I've been one who disassociates. Damir is the complete opposite.

When I was almost ten and Damir was five, our father took the both of us to see *Jurassic Park* despite entreaties by well-meaning friends and family members that we'd be scared out of our pants. My brother spent most of the film nestled face down in dad's lap. When those bird-like creatures were flocking around and over a log, I yelled, "They all look so *fake*." My comment made some adult audience members laugh, but for weeks, my little brother was convinced that hungry Velociraptors hiding under his bed were ready to slice him up and devour him like caviar on a Ritz cracker for their nighttime snack.

Why am I telling you this? Because when I viewed the movie about the massacre in China on the same weekend as Shimizu's *Reincarnation*, I was no longer clinically detached for either film. When a little boy was viciously murdered in the first one, I reacted with horror and revulsion. As for the Japanese flick, each segment produced clues that reincarnation was involved with current cast members, which helped to explain why the director within the film felt so compelled to recreate the particulars of eleven murders by a serial killer – a father who was a college professor (no, not Dick!) – at the now-shuttered Ono Kanko Hotel thirty-five years earlier.

I found it hard to breathe after each film, but as I relaxed later on, I began to question things about myself. For one, why have I always been partial to all things Asian? Music. Culture. Customs. Art. *Shen Yun* dance troupe performances here at Lincoln Center.

At bedtime, I recalled something from my fifth grade geography class years before. Each student had received a brand new textbook about China. To this day I remain unsure why I could never bring myself to put a pencil mark in it. Not even my name. I've since lost that book, or perhaps my mom donated it to some library, but I never spoiled its pristine beauty with classroom notes or any other childish scribbling. I kept it new all term long. It was precious to me. But why?

Another big question soon became overwhelming. Was I, Peter Sergei Petrovich, elder son of two Russian immigrants, a product of reincarnation from someone who'd lived years before, perhaps some young boy who was Chinese? Not a Cossack? The late comedian Jonathan Winters once said, "You come into this world not knowing who you are, and sometimes, if you live long enough, you go out not knowing who you are."

More food for heavy-duty thought, eh?

I did some research. Certain religions say a soul will return if there are remaining sins still to be atoned. An eastern cult decreed that, to attain eventual Nirvana, a person will continue to be reborn, but each new, successive life will be as a lower form.

If that one proved to be true, my boss is on his next-to-last trip. His final appearance on Earth will be as a urinal in a public men's toilet in the Bowery.

To allay any fears you may have about any of this, or about my usually good mental stability, let me assure you things have seemed to return to normal during the last several weeks and with no further occurrences since that one – and only – time.

But I shall be keeping a watchful eye on it just the same.

Very large thanks for that virtual hug, Samantha. It meant a lot. So here's one right back atcha.

Petya, Captain of the Good Ship Dèjá Vu

22.

Dear Disassociated Associate,

    Goldie Loss? LOL. You are one with puns indeed. Ever thought about writing for the New York Times? Newspapers could use more upbeat humour instead of serious articles about disaster and mayhem, drug smuggling and murder.
    I am the type to be highly influenced by violence or horror in movies. Call me squeamish when the decapitation begins and the blood starts to splurt. However, I can see how some would become desensitized after repeated viewings of slicing and dicing. I would point out that *Jurassic Park* is a fictional movie, thus you were conveying the truth that the visuals were fake! The Japanese film *Reincarnation* sounds like a nightmare. I'd be lucky to last through the opening scenes. Psychological thrillers are fine for others, but I'm more into comedies or science fiction. I did watch *Shutter Island*, but it haunted me for weeks, and I now have an aversion to Leonardo DiCaprio because of the role he played. (He is a great actor, but I cringed too watching *Inception* from behind the couch.)
    I don't often think about heaven or the afterlife. Reincarnation seems fascinating, but I don't plan on coming back as a cucumber salad or piñata, one step down from a procrastinating cosmetic salesperson. I don't know why I put procrastination and cosmetics in the same sentence, but you get my drift. The future is bleak if your major concern is getting to work on time so you can dust people with face powder. I feel like a fairy granting wishes, making dreams come true. The fallacy is that many people think they are more beautiful with make-up when real beauty comes from within.
    In regards to your having Chinese "roots" in some past life, it could be possible you have Chinese genes somewhere in your family history. An acquaintance said, "Sam, you have red in your hair. Are you sure you don't have Caucasians in your family tree?" Call me a Twinkie – yellow on the outside, white on the inside!
    I don't think Mr. Johnson was attracted to me because I'm Chinese, but rather because I wore heels that day. I'm positive he

has a shoe fetish because he often compliments females on their shoes and even asked one girl her shoe size. He's in his mid-fifties, I believe. I agree he's probably hit on more women than just me. I hope he chokes on his next teaching evaluation by his superiors, but I'm sure he has tenure. It's pretty hard to get rid of someone like that without formal complaints around his behaviour, and students are likely not going to make waves if the exchange is consensual.

Does Damir work in computer technology? Maybe he should be in computer-generated imagery so he won't get scared in movie theatres, but it does take the fun out of entertainment if you know how things are made. Alas, he was only five when *Jurassic Park* came out. I'm certain he is much braver now.

So I'll wait to hear from you about the progress around my manuscript. Pure or impure, I've come to the conclusion you are a gentleman, which is rare in this day and age. I'd like to send you a box of Goldfish, but by the time it would get to you after being bounced around in a cargo hold, it would be Crumbfish instead.

Bye for now,
Twinkie

23.

Mondays have acquired quite a lousy rep over the years. A record by the Boomtown Rats called "I Don't Like Mondays" was a small hit a few years before I was born, but it was based on a San Diego gal who hated Mondays. I read on Google that a bored, disgruntled teenager decided one Monday morning in 1979 to ditch school and popped away instead with a loaded rifle from her bedroom window. Her target? An elementary school playground across the street from the apartment she shared with her dad. Some of those kids never got to go home to their parents later that day. Monday became more than a bit crappier for them, too.

Enter ever-busy spin doctors who had changed the Monday epithet to "Re-Entry Day." A few poor souls bought into it. Most did not. I was one of them. Mondays still suck.

As I wrapped up my meeting with a publisher-connected client in our small conference room late Monday morning, I removed a copy of Sam's bio, synopsis and sample chapter from my leather folder and slid them across the big table to Bradford M. Worthington, a book editor.

"Brad, I've read a preview of this manuscript. She hooks the reader from page one."

He glanced at the upper left side of the synopsis page where some basic information was typed, smiled and slid it back to me.

"Does she have a brand? Past bestsellers? A huge following on Facebook?"

"No. This is her first serious effort."

"Peter, she's looking at a mighty steep climb, all of it outrageously uphill. And the world of book publishing is changing faster than I can speak. I don't know yet if it's going through a classic renaissance, an overall reconfigured shake-out or a freefall into complete, utter chaos. In my company's case, the big bosses are considering a marketing shift in favor of children's books."

"Why's that?"

"First, our adult and YA titles, along with the non-fiction titles, have not been selling up to expectation. Ongoing losses hurt any business. Secondly, doting, loving parents always seem to want to get their kids off to a flying start in life. To their credit, they never question the hefty price tags of those brief but colorful books. From Miss Chu's 'fiction genre' listed on this, it could be an automatic pass for us in the near future, no matter how great it is. Bottom line.

"However, may I ask if she has representation?"

I looked at him squarely in his eyes. "She could be close to signing with an agent, but she hasn't shared with me who that may be."

"BMW," my unofficial nickname for this fellow who owns three of them, reached for the paper and took a second look. He was doing a speed-read of the plot.

"Tell you what," he said. "As you've helped me make some serious money with your astute financial analyses over the last two years or so in our crap economy, here's what I'll do. I'll read this sample chapter and see how it grabs me. That's a promise. All I ask is that you don't mention it to the aspiring author for the present. No need to get her hopes up, right?"

I nodded. "I appreciate your efforts very much on her behalf. Thanks, Brad."

We shook hands and I escorted him to the elevator as we engaged in some baseball small talk about the season's prospects for the powerhouse Yankees and the hapless Mets.

I had mixed reactions for the rest of the day. It wasn't the knockout success story I had been dreaming of, but BMW said he'd read it. That's hardly a flat-out defeat. Not yet, anyway...

* * *

Wednesday. Hump Day. That evening I felt I had to call my brother, still at work.

"Hello. Thank you for calling Comp-U-World Systems. Damir Petrovich speaking."

"Hello, yourself. Big Brother is calling, kid."

"Hey, Pyotr Sergei! My favorite brotherly ballbuster. How the hell have you been?"

There was a ton of excitement on his end of the line.

"Busy up to my eyeballs. Just like you, probably."

"You better believe it. What's up?"

Untitled Story

"In a word, vacation. I'm looking at getting away from the Rotten Apple for a week or so sometime this summer. Your part of the world works for me. And the shaky tremors out there are no bother. As you know, I live above several subway lines. I live with constant vibrations."

"I think yours are the Beach Boys' type of good vibrations, *tovarish*. L.A. has experienced a few in early April, but we're four hundred miles north, so no problem-o."

"What's your salt mine schedule like?"

"Pretty flexible. The geeks-in-charge gave me a small promotion, which I didn't mention to you in my Christmas card, but I can call my own hours. Plus I get an extra week's vacation. You sure you really want to come out here to boring Oakland?"

"What's wrong with Oakland? You rather I spend a week down in redneck Mississippi? Spearing frogs with the locals in the rivers of good ol' Biloxi instead of 'Silicone' Valley?"

"One *gigs* frogs. And can the sarcasm, you big boob. It's Silicon Valley. S-i-l-i-c-o-n."

"Says you. Besides, I really want to see you again. We can raise some hell. Okay?"

"Yeah, I'm sure we can work something out for June or July. Summer's almost here."

"It's always summer out there. Jeez, after the winter we had – fifty-seven inches of snow. If we had moose, they'd be tickled. Almost a record in the All-Time NYC Snow Sweepstakes."

Damir laughed, the image amusing him. "Good way for you to stay in shape."

"Or get a coronary."

"Get real, you putz. You're way too young for a heart attack." He paused and then asked, "Did you hook up with a bevy of new babes to keep your toes warm at night?"

"A few – and they warmed more than my toes. How about you?"

He groaned. "Every now and again, but it's a challenge to find straight sweeties here."

"Ah, sad is the price one pays for success. Hey, if you should get any baseball tickets for the A's, a pair of good seats behind home plate will do the trick. You can well afford 'em."

"You interested in driving down to 'Dizzyland' too?"

I couldn't resist giving him a hard time. "Magic Mountain might be even more thrilling, provided you can ever work up the nerve to handle all the extra excitement."

"That outrageously expensive, death-defying Six Flags deal for terminal morons? Yeah, don't worry about me. And since you're the goddamn hotshot financial guru, you can pay the freight for any and all amusement parks."

"Okay," I said to keep the boy happy.

"Let's plan on July, then, right after the All-Star break."

"Sounds good, Damir. You still have a house full of destitute roommates?"

"Nope, couldn't stand the constant chaos caused by those wet towel-slapping assholes, so I moved into a neat, quiet condo all by lonesome."

"Congrats."

"Yeah, didn't need 'em anymore to split rent and utilities, either. Immature bastards. And there's a spare bedroom and bath for you at this new place. Spartan and small, but functional."

"Cool. Hey, have you seen any good movies lately?"

"No. You know damn well I was never the movie maven you are. Why?"

"You came up in an e-mail conversation I recently had with a writer in Vancouver. I told her what a brave kid you were when papa took us to see *Jurassic Park* when we were kids."

"You big lump of dreck. You didn't..."

"Uh-huh."

"So what the hell *else* did you tell her? You fill her in on my potty training days, too?"

At that point I was really going to break his chops and invent stuff about his sleeping with that pathetic, raggedy old brown bear, or even about the Polish milkman, but he might get royally pissed off. I laughed and said, "She suggested you switch from computer programming into CGI so results up on the big screen won't terrify you as much."

"I'd say shove it sideways, pal, but believe it or not, that idea has crossed my mind a few times. I'm right near George Lucas's ILM kingdom. We'll talk about it more when you're here. Now, tell me more about this lady writer."

"'Lady Writer' was an early hit for Dire Straits, yes? Hell, why am I asking *you*, Our Lady of Perpetual Nerds? You wouldn't have a freaking clue. Anyhow, she's Chinese-Canadian and has the all the makings of a damn fine author. I've read her first novel."

"How did you meet her? Have you visited her in British Columbia?"

"I've never met her, little brother. Only corresponded with her on the Internet."

Damir sounded incredulous. "You shittin' me?"

"Nope, she's a college student, and all of twenty. After she'd posted a sample chapter on a popular writers' website, I posted my comments. She's since put up several more chapters and has about fifty responses to date, all positive. She's real good, but I don't think she knows how good she really is. I was totally mesmerized by her talent."

"Are you considering a side trip to Canada while you're out here? Maybe check her out in person, you horny bastard?" Damir sounded much too enthusiastic.

"That hasn't even crossed my mind. And are you also in the matchmaking biz these days? I haven't mentioned anything to her about a trip. Besides, it's not that kind of relationship. I don't know what she looks like."

"G'wan. That sounds like total bullshit to me..."

"No, it's true, but she must be quite a hottie because one of her professors began hitting on her. She brushed it off, saying it was because she was wearing high heels and that he must have a serious foot fetish."

Damir laughed, but it sounded more like a snort. "Sick-o dickweeds, those professorial dudes. But why haven't you asked her for any photos?"

"Because I don't care. There are enough sex-starved beauties in New York to keep yours pretty damn busy. Ask me sometime about Lucy, the hot Mexican tamale. She'd cornered me in the men's room after hours about two weeks ago."

"And?"

"For me to know and for you to have a wet dream about."

"Enough about your sex life, real or imagined. I gotta go," Damir said, bringing the call to its conclusion. "Some beanbag's been knocking like mad on my office door."

"Okay. We'll talk again. Or e-mail me. *Das vedanya*, kid."

"Yeah, Pyotr. And get her friggin' picture – for *me*. My insatiable curiosity's aroused."

"And that's the only thing aroused? Or insatiable?"

The connection clicked off, but it felt good to have my vacation plans shaping up well so far. And it'll be super to raise some hell with Damir again. It's been way too "Damn" long.

24.

I'd been feeling an itch between my shoulder blades all day. I don't often get the itch like that unless something monumental is going to happen. I hadn't heard from Peter for a week since I sent him the manuscript and synopsis. I knew that my author's bio was pretty thin. Who would take a risk on a newbie writer?

At first, I thought the itch meant I was going to get A's on my term essays. I was very pleased indeed when I received top marks; however, the itch persisted. Then I was voted Best New Employee and given a blue ribbon to wear at work. I would add I was the only new employee besides pimply Dale who quit after his first shift, but hey, one doesn't look a gift horse in the mouth.

Still that blasted itch continued to bother me despite applying lotion and the use of a backscratcher. Damn it anyway!

Something was up, but I couldn't place my finger on it. And what was happening with Peter? I didn't want to call or email him if he didn't respond first. I didn't want to look needy or desperate for attention. Was he in a car accident? Had he come down with a deadly disease? Or had he somehow disappeared off the face of the earth?

25.

I can't believe how fast things pile up. Samantha writes. I want to respond ASAP. What happens? I get buried in the effluvial waste of my daily activities. Tonight I took one step back from the bathroom mirror and asked the guy in the reflection, "Are you getting rich from this?" He just lowered his head and kept shaking it slowly. At least he didn't collapse in hysterics.

Okay. Enough procrastinating. Time to reach out to that Canadian gal...

Subject: Progress Report

Hey, Twinkie ~

Peter Pan has been busy last week, but I did have a chance to get your material to Bradford Worthington, the first victim. The editor indicated his company was considering publication of only kids' books in the near future, but promised to give your opening chapter a read, although he asked me not to say anything to you so that your hopes weren't dashed to the rocks if he should say no. I never signed my name to any contract holding me to that, but please try to keep it all in perspective before you jump for joy.

He provided a brief overview of the quick-changing world of publishing, including the onslaught of e-books. I kinda knew this as I notice Nooks and Kindles on the subway every day. It seems any space cadet not texting or blabbing away on a cell phone is using them. A few years ago, I'd read how *The Help*, Kathryn Stockett's first novel, was rejected by sixty-two book publishers before the sixty-third scored with a major bestseller and a solid movie project deal that produced one Academy Award winning performance and several other nominations. Whatever were all those other guys *thinking*? I'll have to hedge my bets here. It would seem when the Good Lord handed out brains, they thought He said trains and were all waiting down at the depot. Duh.

Untitled Story

You mentioned an actor that had spooked you – and with a lingering aversion to the guy, no less. I also saw *Shutter Island* a while back. I didn't think he was all that bad in it, but despised him in *The Aviator*. What were studio heads thinking when they cast that baby-faced cherub in the difficult role of an aging Howard Hughes? Damn, I nearly laughed my rear end off.

Speaking of "Damn," I phoned him last Wednesday and set up a tentative one-week vacation at his new condo in Oakland in July. It'll be after baseball's All-Star Game, but I haven't got exact dates yet. Haven't seen the boy for over two years now, and his language has gotten somewhat saltier. I wanted to ask him if he eats with that potty mouth. Anyway, I mentioned the CGI type of work you had suggested. He said he's been mulling over such a move in his head. GMTA, it seems.

And with all this speaking of heads, you claim to have some *red* hair? LMAO. Is it real or out of a bottle, Ms. Punk-Rocker?

Crumbfish, Samantha? Great to dump into the borscht. Send a bag. Please... (Snailmail addy is attached.)

Rumblefish Crumblefish Petey

P.S.: Mr. Lonely Hearts in Oakland requests a recent photo of the authoress for his collection. Thx in advance.

26.

After receiving Pete's latest message, I hunted for a photograph that did me justice and found a family photo taken last Christmas. I cut the others out of the picture and glued the image of me on a blank card. I decided to handwrite him a note to post in the mail:

Dear Petey,

Seriously, why would your brother want a photo of me? What did you say about *moi*? Anyway, I'm sending you this cutout of me from last December. You can't make out the red hair because of the indoor lighting, but if you squint, you might see my brown eyes. Twinkies aside, my skin is actually caramel—the colour, not the candy.

You're going to be in Oakland in July? As a coincidence, I'm applying for a scholarship to attend a two-day writing conference at a hotel in San Francisco in July. Get this: to apply you have to write 250 words about why writing is important to you and/or why you write. I decided not to write about literature as an art form, but rather write about my love affair with writing. Here's what I have so far…

> *I am not a person of means, but a hardworking soul who at the age of six won a poetry contest at my school. Most children in grade one are just starting to learn the alphabet. I prepared my poem and recited it in front of the class.*
>
> *Blossoms open, petals fall*
> *White flesh of an apple*
> *Sweet not bitter*
> *I taste you*
>
> *They applauded and I received a blue ribbon, which hangs on my bedroom wall to this day. I*

Untitled Story

didn't write that poem for fame or fortune, but rather because I felt things deeply, best expressed through words and that is why I write.

Well, at least it's a beginning. It is a true story, but what I didn't include is that my mother dressed me up like an apple to recite the poem at a school assembly. Some kid threw his apple at me, and everyone laughed. Kids can be cruel!

So the "first victim" is reading my story? I feel the tension, the thrill of the hunt. Saliva drips down my chin as I smell the scent of victory. Well, maybe I'm ahead of the plot, but they always tell you to visualize your dreams. Alas, if you can't dream, how will you ever succeed? I'm not the most patient person as far as waiting to hear more, but however this plays out, I'm game.

Cheerio,
Caramel Apple

27.

When I read Samantha's letter, complete with the enclosed stunning photo, I laughed hard at her reaction to Damir's unusual request for her picture. Who on God's green Earth could possibly know why? Maybe he wants to see for himself that she's not a mummified ancient goddess from some Inuit tribe.

I was pleased to hear her latest news and replied via e-mail:

Subject: Progress (?) Report #2

Hey, Blue Ribbon, Candied Caramel Apple ~

Your letter arrived bearing great news. If your entry wins that scholarship trip to San Francisco and if our dates in Northern California should actually overlap, we'll finally be able to have that cup of coffee – on me. (But not the spilled kind. I know your track record in that department.)

Your application sample reads very well so far. It has the ring of honesty. Genuine and unique. Ah likes it, so good luck.

Your photo was a knockout. As for the reason "Damn" wants it? I'm thoroughly in the dark. My electricity is shut off. No candles available. The boy tends to get excitable every now and then. I guess our discussion about you must have created something "new" for him, but neither of us may ever know. However, if I ever *do* manage to wring the truth out of him, you'll be the second one to know – after me. And I plan to hold off sending it to keep him in suspense.

Finally, here's a progress report of sorts for you. Last week I was able to get your material to two other publishing reps, both editors. One is female, the other male (associate). The bad news first.

The gent wouldn't take it, saying the submission was not delivered by an agent. He didn't get all huffy about it, but I still feel he was overly rigid in his old-school attitude. Screw him. Maybe I'll set him up with a small loss on his next investment. He can afford it. On the other hand, the lady was far more open and amenable, but her "acceptance speech" was patterned much the same as the first fellow's recent mantra.

Her bottom line? "No promises." Let's see where it goes from here...

Peter, your designated temp agent

28.

Dear in the Dark,

Maybe you should ask your brother if he collects photos of girls he doesn't know because he doesn't have one of his own. What will he do with my picture anyway? Carry it in his wallet or post it on his Facebook page as "The Girl I Don't Know and Have Never Met"? And people will leave comments such as "Is that *The Girl Who Got Away*"? or "The relationship you never had either?" I'll be named the Mystery Woman who never went to Damnation.

But seriously, if he's your brother, how bad can he be? Or is that up for debate? As far as I know, the Silicon Valley isn't known for crimes other than perhaps hacking or causing thumb fatigue by extensive video gaming. You're not in league with the Yakuza or Mafia as far as I can tell. I believe everyone has faults, but I confess I haven't seen any psychological imbalance or illegal activity on your part.

So I submitted my contest entry for the scholarship. Fingers crossed and legs, too. Under no circumstances would I use my body to get ahead. The idea of being fondled by Mr. Johnson makes me nauseous even thinking about. I thought about wearing slippers to class so he'd stop looking at my $99 pumps. Or ask all the girls to go barefoot to see how turned on he'd get. Everyone in my class knows about his fetish after he showed us a slide show of his shoe collection. Just kidding!

The contest results will be announced soon. To have a coffee with you would be awesome, and I'll try not to be a *drip* if we do actually meet up. LOL. If I don't make it to California, it'll be a setback, but my life is full of those. Life isn't about always being successful. You have to roll with it.

Case in point, the first rejection to my manuscript. "Oh, yes, it was a beautiful story, well-written and deep with metaphors, but you don't have an agent." Why do publishers do that? I can see how having an agent means a story has been vetted before it reaches a publisher, but there are many fine writers who do not have an agent, but are brilliant. Even publishers can miss hitting one out of the park.

I may die an unknown author, but I hope deep in my heart that someone out there is ready to take on *The Boy Who Got Away*, and by hook or by crook, I'm going to find that person.

Someone in my creative writing class asked the professor about self-publishing which is becoming more popular. You know what he said? "It's not part of my curriculum." He won't even talk about it. What's the point of the class if you can't talk about publishing?

So I put up my hand and said, "E-books are taking more and more of the market. Do you think printed books will one day be eliminated?"

He looked at me and said, "I don't know. I'm only a professor." Oh, god. He was too timid to even offer an opinion. I mean, he can talk for eons about Shakespeare or Chaucer or dissect a novel, but he doesn't discuss anything about working as a writer. No advice at all on submitting to magazines or journals either. I'm going to write a letter to the head of the English Department to put publishing, distribution, and marketing in the course outline. You can't exist as a writer if no one knows it.

Some people want to get rich or famous, but success is relative. When I had my article published in the school newspaper, I was happy as a clam. Small victories are stepping stones to larger ones. Somewhere in there is a lesson learned. You have to crawl before you can walk or run. Then the sky is the limit!

Flying high over Vancouver (Writer on helium)

I signed off my computer and put on my coat to leave for an evening shift at the drugstore. I felt as if I were living two lives. I was a student working part-time as a cosmetician, but also a dreamer of reaching new heights in the future.

This latest correspondence with Pete now gave me hope and anticipation of new opportunities. Writing back and forth with him was an escape from my blue days. I hadn't yet called to hear his voice, but maybe someday.

29.

Even before Sam's latest e-mail musings arrived, signed off with an overabundance of hope, the black dog of depression had set in, complete with a nagging headache that throbbed as a dull ache throughout the working day. I know that I – and many others now on the Wordsmiths website – have heaped legitimate praise on her work, but what if it should come to nothing? How would I feel if her dreams of pursuing a writing career were dashed to tiny pieces on the rocks of a stormy coastline, that being the nature of the cutthroat world of publishing?

After work, I decided to make a run over to Barnes & Noble in Union Square as I knew they'd stocked Anne Leroy's book, *Your Novel: From First Draft to Publication – and Beyond*. She was not only a successful agent, but one of my financial clients. I found a hardcover copy and quickly flipped through its 250 pages filled with informative how-to tips and superb advice in navigating the complex maze on the road to having one's work in print.

Without hesitation, I purchased it, cost be damned. It was as much for Samantha's use as for mine, since I was the bold idiot having led the rah-rah charge right from the very beginning of this insane odyssey, and one that I didn't wish to see end for her in disappointment.

Skipping dinner, I dived headlong into it. I devoured and digested Anne's words better than any gourmet meal – until it dawned on me: I had no place in Vancouver to ship this because dopey me had tossed out the envelope with her return address…

Subject: Undeliverable Gift

Dear High on Helium ~

You made me laugh at your comments about "Damn." You wrote, "How bad can he be?" That's rich – and highly debatable. From all the video games he plays, it's a miracle he still has tips on his thumbs. And for years I've been telling the boy he couldn't rent a date. Either gender. Do you think that he and some of your inept, opinion-less profs might share a common genetic link?

The jury is out on two of the three editors. Because my literary agent friend Anne Leroy hasn't dropped by the office lately, I got the bright idea to buy her book for you. Sorry to say, agents are a necessary evil, just as they are important buffers between studio heads and frustrated screenwriters in Tinsel Town.

Anyway, Anne's book is full of great stuff that you'll need to know. Like, if your novel is picked up and published, how will you as a college student be able to support sales? Will you be able to tour Canada and the U.S. for book signings? Doing television and radio interviews? Newspapers and magazines, too? And how will Mama Chu react to your gallivanting all around the world in pursuit of success while ignoring your ongoing education?

As an added (and most unfortunate) note, your very disorganized e-pal seems to have misplaced your address, so I need your help. Desperately. So could you please send it to me again?

Possibly Permanently Perplexed Peter

* * *

    I stared intently at Sam's photo, which now occupied a prominent place on my desk. The picture looked more candid than posed, and her smile spoke volumes about her personality while her eyes seemed to sparkle and dance. Although it was taken from the waist up, there was no mistaking that Samantha Chu was one tiny wisp of a gal.
    As I'd written to her, I had delayed sending it to Damir just to make him wait, but now I decided today would be the day.
    I scanned her photo, created a jpeg and forwarded it to him with the warning he should treat this "gift" with great respect.
    I also added a postscript to ask the reason he felt he needed to have it.
    Less than five minutes had elapsed when I received an incoming text:

Damir: HOLY FLYIN' *FRIJOLES*, BATMAN!!!

Gathering the photo knocked his socks off, I texted him right back.

Peter: That didn't take you long, Boy Wonder...

Damir: There are priorities in this life, you booger, and then there are *priorities*!

Peter: So this convinces you that she's not an old bag lady.

Damir: Are you freakin' nuts? She's a beauty queen!

Peter: Well, now you can add Miss Canada to your "collection" of the gals you'll never have.

Damir: WTF? I requested it for YOU, dumbass.

Peter: Huh?

Damir: Here you are, corresponding like a wild man, but no guts to ask for her pic. Sad.

Peter: I told you our relationship wasn't like that.

Damir: Uh-huh. Sure. Maybe it should be. So consider this an early Christmas gift from me.

Peter: She'll be flattered – and relieved – to learn you think of her as a holiday commodity.

Damir: I am most pleased to accept your very sincere "Thank you." Gotta run. Ta-ta.

He disappeared into cyberspace before I could type out her comments about his need to get a life. Anyway, time enough later on, I suppose...

I pondered Damir's comments. Was I blind to Samantha's attractiveness? Not really, but I was uncertain if anything would ever come of our relationship. E-mailing back and forth across a big continent was a comfortable distance. No commitments. But if she and I should meet up in sunny California, I'd consider bringing Damir along.

The boy really did need to get out more.

30.

Wow! I blinked at Pete's email. He bought me a book and was willing to ship it to Canada? I visualized him arriving at my doorstep with book in hand. It would be interesting explaining to my parents about a stranger who appeared out of nowhere looking for me.

I realized I'd developed a sense of trust with Pete. It dawned on me that we were not only pen pals, but also bonding over a book.

Dear Mr. Postman,

How kind of you to offer to send me a book. Any advice on navigating the world of publishing and marketing is much appreciated. I'm a newbie to the nuts and bolts of the industry.

Speaking of "Dateless Damn," he must get out more. He needs to leave the computer chips at home and meet some people.

Has he tried speed dating? I hear that's the rage right now. I personally haven't tried it as it takes me about a minute to think of something to say to a stranger – and the clock is ticking the whole time. I guess you'd call me a slow dater.

I have a friend who fell in love with a guy through an online dating service. They hit it off right away, got hitched and are living in Seattle. The only complaint she has is that he's involved with chat groups online more often than having verbal conversations with real people. I mean they talk and all that, but he's on the computer way too much. She's afraid he'll be tempted to meet other girls on the Internet and dump her.

I didn't know what to say to her other than "Buyer Beware." She bought into this relationship, packed her bags, and moved to a different country. Maybe she should have researched the product more thoroughly before spending time, effort, and money. More importantly, I don't want her heart to be broken.

Thanks for thinking of me by purchasing the book. I'm attaching my address.

Slow-dating Sam

After I signed off, I had a moment. I felt the heebie-jeebies that Pete was going to all this trouble and my book might not be good enough. I'd had doubts before, but was I putting all my eggs in one basket that he would find me a publisher? Should I be looking elsewhere and if I did, would he decide not to help me out?

Surely, he was attempting to aid me, but was it worth it for him? What was he really getting out of the deal? Was there a catch or obligation on my part? What should I do for him in return?

That's when I got the idea to call him long-distance. But didn't I need a good reason? I didn't want to call out of the blue and have nothing to say.

31.

Sam's e-mail was waiting as soon as I got home. "Dateless Damn," she wrote. That gal's got one neat sense of humor.

She mentioned the latest trend of speed dating. I'd heard it referenced on TV a few times. Then I thought how fast Lucy would open a "conversation" to a complete stranger: "Hey, man, how 'bout you wanna come an' screw your brains out weeth me?"

The story about her married friend now in Seattle gave me a chuckle. Sometimes love is blind to the fault of one's partner that can grow into potentially bigger issues later on.

After I'd prepared the Customs slip requirement and book package for mailing, I sent it off the next day. The Grand Central Station Post Office on Lexington at 44th was near my worksite, but I didn't get back to Sam for a week and felt lousy about it. There was an ongoing crisis to attend to at the office, which took up an inordinate amount of time and energy. I prayed for the eventual day when the entire damn stock market would quit thinking it was a wicked rollercoaster ride at Coney Island.

My landline rang as I was pouring myself a drink.

"Hello?"

A tentative female voice spoke. "Peter?"

I took a wild guess. "Samantha?"

"The one and only."

A bolt of energy shot through my exhausted body. "Hi! How are ya?"

"I'm fine..."

"What a great surprise to hear your voice. Finally..."

"Yours, too. The James Dean guy."

"Ah, but *this* one's alive 'n' kickin'."

I could hear a faint giggle on her end. "I just wanted to say thanks for all your help."

"Glad to do it."

"Any updates on possible publishers?"

"Unfortunately, Brad passed on your book yesterday despite liking your sample a lot. 'Professionally written' were his exact words. But his company is struggling hard to survive these days.

He was afraid that the bosses would refuse to take any chances on someone without an established track record. Hey, I figure it's their loss."

"No sale, but his words were kind."

"The industry is a rough one. Kind of like mine. Remember when you wrote I wasn't in the Mafia and had no bad traits or habits? Well, both businesses are a form of gambling. It's not like I play the ponies or hang out in casinos, but I sometimes 'gamble' on my own financial tips that I provide for others. Sometimes I win. Other times not."

"I never thought of it that way," she said with a touch of surprise.

"Same with the book world. They'll be investing in a product never knowing with crystal ball accuracy whether it'll end up being a bestseller or a flop. I once read that profits from ten percent of famous writers cover the losses incurred by the other ninety percent. That is the nature of the beast, dear lady."

"First cousins to the music and movie industries, too."

"Same difference," I said, more or less agreeing with her comment.

"*C'est la vie.* But I did want to thank you for buying Anne Leroy's book for me. That was so sweet."

"It should get there soon."

"That's fine, but I hope it wasn't too expensive to send."

"Nothing I couldn't handle." I paused to swallow hard. "That photo of you was so cool."

"You think?"

"Yeah. I finally sent the jpeg to 'Dateless Damn,' as you so aptly referred to him. It blew the kid away. I think he walked around babbling and bumping into things for the rest of the day."

"Did you ask why he wanted it?"

"You will *not* believe his answer. The boy requested it for me because, according to him, I was too chicken to ask for one for myself."

"He said that?"

"Yeah. He texted me that I should reassess my relationship with you. I knew damn well he was full of it right up to his baby brown eyeballs, but he bailed out before I could tell him to get a life. Or even to drop dead."

"Am I really that undesirable?"

"Author Oscar Wilde once said, 'I can resist anything except temptation.' But I cannot resist teasing you, so please don't take it personally. I was only kidding."

She laughed and said, "You two are too much. You should take your show on the road."

Then Sam sucked in a long breath. "Pete, I have good news. I won the contest! I'll be going to San Francisco!"

Again, I couldn't resist the urge to tease her. "Then our road show will be coming to you this summer, live from Oakland..." But I was really beyond amazed. "That is fantastic news."

Sam became even more exuberant as we chatted, and we talked a little more before she ended the call. We no longer had a so-called long-distance relationship – I was finally going to meet the fair damsel.

After hanging up, I was forced to ask myself a more serious question: Just how will I ever get to sleep *now*?

32.

I was definitely out of my comfort zone in regards to initiating a rendezvous with Pete. I must really like him, I thought. I was excited to tell Pete details about my trip to coordinate with his trip to Oakland.

He said he could make the drive from Oakland to San Francisco and even hire Damir as a chauffeur. I was curious about meeting Damir. He seemed like a real character.

The scholarship paid for my travel, accommodation and conference fee. June passed quickly with emails flying between Peter and me with the odd phone calls in between.

I dug out an old suitcase and packed my essentials. The weather forecast was hot and sunny for the entire weekend. The day of my departure came. My mother drove me to the airport in the early morning. My jewelry set off the metal detector at the security check and I thought they were going to arrest me when the alarm went off, but I boarded the plane, leaving on schedule.

I spent the relatively short flying time reading the last few chapters of Anne's book, which I hadn't got around to finish earlier. Then the plane set down on a runway in San Francisco. I took a taxi to the hotel and lined up to check in. There were a lot of hotel guests checking in because of the conference.

Finally, I got my room keycard and took the elevator to the sixth floor. My suite was small, but it was my own. I kicked off my shoes and rubbed my toes against the plush carpet. I looked out the window across the bay. I had arrived in more ways than one.

* * *

A male voice answered. "Hello?"
"It's Samantha." I held the phone close to my ear.
"Oh, hi. This is Damir."
"I've heard a lot about you."
"Oh, yeah? If you heard it from my brother, they're all lies. He gets his jollies spreading nasty rumors about me that he can't substantiate."

"Is Pete there?"

There was a rustling sound on the other end and I could overhear talking. "Hey, bro. The eagle has landed."

A deeper voice came on the line. "If it isn't Caramel from Canada. Hope you had a good flight into this very hot part of the world."

"Peter, it's summer in Canada, too."

He laughed. "When I think of Vancouver, I think of c-o-l-d and s-n-o-w. Anyway, Damir has been itching to meet you. He printed out your picture and posted it all over his bedroom."

"Oh, god. Is he a perv?"

Pete laughed. "I chain him down at night so he doesn't go out and harass the neighbors. Say, are you free? Lunch, perhaps? Coffee, at the very least..."

"There's an introductory event and a keynote speaker tonight. But if you have me back by seven, it's doable."

"Okay if I bring Damir along? He's the one with the Ferrari."

"Ah, sure. A Ferrari?" I pictured Damir as a lonely guy with a clunker. How did such an unsociable guy end up with a Ferrari? He was full of surprises.

"Didn't I tell you? He's loaded. Meet you outside your hotel in about an hour."

I felt a shiver of delight and said goodbye. I slipped on some nice heels and a denim dress with a short hemline. I brushed my hair and checked my mascara in the mirror and took the elevator downstairs ready to meet the dynamic duo.

I checked my watch every thirty seconds as I observed the cars speeding by. I wondered if I should have gone back to my room to change my shoes. Was I overdressed? Maybe I should have worn sneakers and shorts. Oh, well. I'd have to make the best of it. Then I saw a red Ferrari with a blond driver and dark-haired passenger beside him. They waved and pulled up to the curb. Peter got out of the car and gave me a hug. He was taller than I thought, but I felt like I knew him for years.

"Don't I get a frigging hug, too?" asked an expectant but sad-faced Damir.

"Loser," said Peter, "you're only the chauffeur. Get hug, lose tip. Worse, lose job. Words of wisdom to live by, foolish boy." He opened the door and bowed. "Your chariot awaits, young lady.

And that denim dress suits you perfectly."

I beamed at his compliment as I got in the backseat. Pete rode upfront where he could stretch out his long legs. Peter and Damir got into a discussion of the best place to eat.

Pete's suggestion was lightning fast. "If you're paying, big shot, let's go to Saison."

"But maybe Sam would like a burger and fries." Damir glanced at me in the rear view mirror.

"If I may interrupt," I said, "how is it that Damn has this car and no girlfriend? This car is a girl magnet."

"I've only had it for a week. As for the ladies, none of them are as hot as you."

"Well, that's a nice thing to say, Blondie. Don't you think so, Pete?"

Pete slouched down in his seat and grimaced. "There he goes, Sam. Little brother begins hitting on another pretty lady. As usual."

"Hell, Pete. I was just making casual conversation. Jeez."

"Yeah, as casual as a dog in heat," Pete said under his breath. After an uncomfortable pause, he turned again to Damir. "Classy gals like Samantha don't like that stuff. You are so out of your league." He shook his head and muttered, "Pathetic."

Damir pulled up to the curb at a burger joint.

"Really, Damn?" asked Pete. "*This* is where you take a lady?"

"They have great lunch specials. I've eaten here before. C'mon."

The diner was a nice family restaurant with comfortable booths and exuded the typical American ambience I've read about and seen in movies. I took a seat and Pete squeezed next to me while Damir sat facing us. The menus were extensive. I decided on fish and chips and a cola. Pete ordered the more expensive grilled salmon platter. He turned to me and said with a grin, "Hey, I'm still a growing boy."

That didn't seem to hold true for his much thinner brother who ordered only a plain hamburger. When it arrived, Damir could only pick at it.

"Damn, why aren't you eating?" I asked. "I thought you liked this restaurant."

Then he surprised me.

"Samantha, I could stare at your eyes forever," he said as if in a trance.

Peter said, "It's not her eyes that you've been staring at. So would you kindly stop lying already?" He looked at me and rolled his eyes.

I laughed and then the two of us turned toward his brother. "You really should get out more," we said in unison. I kept laughing.

"There's a real popular T-shirt in New York for women," Peter said. "It reads 'No Eye Contact, Please.' Think I'll have to buy one for Sam now..."

Damir was sweet and charming. Peter came off somewhat as a crabby old curmudgeon, but the repartee between them was hilarious. I thought it was part of their act as brothers.

At least that was what I thought in that moment. As the afternoon progressed, Pete backed off gradually from any meaningful conversation while Damir came alive more and more in his own unique way of attempting to impress me about himself. He seemed to be hungrier for attention than he was for food. My intuition told me, however, that Pete was holding back his emotions. What I didn't realize was that his often barbed, sarcastic comments might be the tip of an iceberg.

Once our stomachs were full and we were ready to go, I took out my camera so that we could snap a few photos. Damir took one of us. Pete stood, placed a decent tip on the table for our waitress and paid the check at the register. On the way to the car, he held out his open hand to Damir. His brother was taken by surprise.

"What's that mean, huh?"

"Give me the keys. I'm driving back." To me, Pete said, "You ride in front with me."

Damn objected because the car was so new.

Pete gave him the evil eye. "Little brother, be grateful I don't tie you to the rear bumper."

Damir handed over the keys. I must say I relished the new authority in Pete's voice and actions, and I felt excited to be riding next to him.

At the hotel's entrance, Peter got out, opened my door and escorted me inside the lobby while Damir remained with his precious Ferrari. We took the elevator.

"These couple of hours were way too short, Sam," Pete said over the familiar refrain of Gotye's "Somebody That I Used to Know" on the elevator's speakers. As the doors slid closed behind us, he added, "I don't wish to monopolize all your time at this conference, but would it be in the realm of possibility for us to meet once more?"

"The hotel has a complimentary breakfast for guests in the morning. I'm sure I can sneak you in without a problem."

Pete's face lit up. "Then I'll rent a car later and be here at eight sharp tomorrow."

"Without Damn?"

"I'll leave him where he belongs – in front of a computer."

The elevator doors opened, and he walked me to the door of my suite. Peter hugged me warmly. Then he leaned in close to place a polite kiss on my forehead. He drew back, paused for several seconds and gave me one more on my lips. Then a second longer one that made my feet tingle.

When I opened my eyes again, he was already walking to the elevator. Once there, he turned to give me a smile and a final wave. I did the same, in slow-motion.

And then he was gone...

* * *

Trying to fall asleep was difficult, if not impossible. Tossing and turning were the order of this long night as so many thoughts were racing around inside my head. I needed to sort them into one tidy package, but that was not to be. I didn't want to pull an all-nighter, only to fall asleep on one of the lecturers the following day. Still, I couldn't stop thinking about the soulful kisses Pete gave me outside the room.

No sooner than I had dozed, the phone rang, breaking the dreamlike, peaceful silence of the morning. I was hoping to hear Pete's voice, but it was only the automated wake-up call I'd requested, giving me sufficient time to shower and dress.

I waited patiently outside and in the lobby. When it seemed as if Pete might be a no-show, I tried to call Damir's home, but only the answering machine picked up. I texted Peter, but there wasn't any response to that, either. Was he all right? Did he get into an accident? As usual, I began to worry. I ate breakfast alone, but without appetite or enthusiasm.

The conference kept me busy for the rest of the weekend. I left a message on Pete's cell to call back, but again there was no contact, which I found rather odd. I flew back to Vancouver feeling confused. I sent Pete an email, but instead I received one several days later, from his brother, which provided details about an unfortunate incident that had occurred...

Dearest Samantha,

I did a very unscrupulous thing for which I trust you'll eventually forgive me. During my brother's short stay here, I searched his luggage while he was in the shower to obtain your e-mail address. I found it in a small notebook he uses.

At first, I was thoroughly entranced only by your gorgeous photo, and then to have met you in person and finding you even more captivating than your picture, my whole world turned upside-down! I knew my boring life might never again be the same. That's the most important thing I have to tell you.

The second is that my boorish behavior set my unpredictable brother into a rage. He left the same day we all had lunch and is back in NY, but not before punching me in the face. I didn't know the guy had it in him! I can still hear his furious words when we got back to my condo and he began shoving me hard: "Why did you have to make a complete ass out of yourself in front of Samantha? And you have the unmitigated gall to call *me* horny? You lowlife hypocrite!"

OK. I was wrong to hit on you, especially in his company, but the physical chemistry on my end went wild. Berserk. Nuts. Wacko. Totally out of control, just like TILT on some old-time pinball game. I admit that upfront to you and am truly sorry about it as far as I can be. I didn't know he had any real feelings for you. Honest.

Remember it was me, his kid brother, who requested your photo for *him*. I kept pushing him to examine any of those feelings that might be resting dormant deep within his own psyche. Man, did I push a hot button!

Untitled Story

I checked into the local ER for bruises, bleeding and to have my jaw checked out. When the docs asked me what had happened, I lied and said I'd been mugged, but didn't get a good look at the guy. They didn't push for any more answers after that. I spent four or five hours at the hospital. They x-rayed my jaw and gave me stitches. When they determined I was more or less all right, they discharged me and told me to rest and to file a police report, but I never went to the cops.

Again, I apologize for coming on so strong – and childishly. I'd never met someone like you. Ever! Please, please forgive me, Sam, but I do care about you. Keep in touch if you want to. And if not, I will understand. Believe that.

But I will never forget the very special lady you are.

With much (remaining) affection,
Damir Petrovich

* * *

I was aware that Peter had not sent me any new emails – but now I feared contacting him. A cold shiver ran through me. Did I really know Pete at all? After our many humorous and amiable emails and phone calls, I never had the slightest hint that he might possess a violent streak. Each time I read Damir's email, my heart continued to throb and sink further inward, and then I began to cry – and for days afterward, it seemed like.

Dear Damir,

I'm so sorry if I caused conflict between you and your brother and I want Pete to know that as well. This whole sequence of events has gone very badly and I feel anguish over it.

I'm also writing you because I'm terrified about Pete. Has he a history of violence? I emailed him, but have had no response. Has he spoken to you since the incident? Do you know if he's okay? I can't believe he hit you after the gentle kisses he gave me at the hotel.

I am flattered you are attracted to me, and I admit I flirted back as well, but it was all harmless fun. I did have unspoken feelings for Pete, but after this latest news, I don't know what to say. I can't tame a lion.

Sincerely yours,
Sam

33.

Dear Bro,

    I know you're still angry about the Samantha incident, but for the tenth freakin' time, I'm apologizing. I took the liberty of filling Sam in on what happened because you haven't been writing her.
    She apologized for any unintentional conflict between us she might have sparked. She's a beautiful, caring lady. What else can I say? She's worried about you despite your abusive actions toward *moi*. So get on the goddam phone and call the lady! Okay?

Geesh,
Damn

34.

The picture of us that Samantha had e-mailed as we'd sat smiling and almost snuggling in the diner's booth had joined her original photo on my desk after I'd printed it on quality paper stock. As I kept thinking about how all the possibilities that could have existed with that sweet woman and how fast they were beginning to unravel, courtesy of my out-of-control, conniving and manipulating sibling, I reached for and ripped up the other jpeg I'd printed out of the three of us, taken by the waitress.

Perhaps I was too hasty. It occurred to me that I should reprint it, editing out Sam and me as a keeper. Then I could post Damir's portion and throw darts at his mug all "Damn" day...

The more I read his never-ending streams of alcohol-fueled babbling, assorted gibberish and convoluted bullshit, the more infuriated I got. I'd been licking my emotional wounds for several weeks, only to have this immature relative pour salt into them. That was about to end.

I sat in front of my PC screen and lined up his e-addy, but this time, with a bcc to Sam:

Subject: THIS MEANS WAR!

What's all this 'bro' crap, you moron? Real siblings don't pull what you did. Perhaps you're only my *half*-brother, courtesy of some milkman from a quarter-century ago. Think about that, pal...

So, you've been filling Sam in on our little argument? And how did you learn how to contact her? By going through my stuff like a conniving little weasel. Didn't you think I knew what you'd done? You left my notebook open, idiot. If you would have asked, I may have supplied her info to you at the time.

Now? Never.

If you're reading this sober, allow me to recap those unfortunate events for your feeble mind.

Untitled Story

You came on to Sam from beginning to end like a runaway freight train. Nothing I said was able to derail you. You couldn't take a simple hint from either of us. So thoroughly absorbed in your own pathetic self, you never noticed how pissed off I got. But it didn't end at lunch, did it? When we got back to your place, you started to belt down drink after drink like the country had decided overnight to reinstate Prohibition. I asked you to dial back on the boozing, but you kept ignoring me. That would've been all right by itself, but then you had to get rowdy and loud, slurring your words about how you had to take Sam away from me, just like you did a few other gals a couple of years ago. You're the grand master of the old 4Fs: Find 'em. Feel 'em. Fuck 'em. Forget 'em.

First off, jackass, Samantha isn't *mine*. I don't *own* her. Despite my high opinion of her – and her talent – we are not a couple, but maybe we should be just to add to your pity party and otherwise self-imposed misery. Hey, we shared several wonderful kisses by her room. I never felt closer to any human being. And I'd do it all over again in a NY minute, so eat your jealous little heart out.

Second, about those other ladies back in the day? Once they realized what a loser you were, they headed straight for the hills like the devil himself was hot on their heels. Did any ever come back to me? Noooooooo. Enough of that wild Petrovich family in one lifetime for those poor, lost souls.

What I'll never understand is why you started shoving me around, or at least attempting to. You charged into me and smashed your pie-eyed face into my shoulder. And what did you get for all your trouble? A little bloody nose and a fall to the hardwood floor when you slipped. What a colossal dumbass. I haven't hit a soul since I defended you against that bully in grade school for stealing the lunch money Mama gave you. What did I get for my actions? Big trouble with the principal who called up Papa to come see him after school, only later to get a beating from him, too. Ever wonder why I became a lifelong pacifist after that? Goddamn Russian justice...

You're no longer the brother I'd once loved. This trip showed me you've changed. Drastically. Your drinking is out of control, just like your other excesses. "Nothing exceeds like excess." Isn't that what Elvira told Tony Montana in *Scarface*? It wouldn't surprise me to learn you're snorting white powder straight up your nose just like all the rest of those geeky cokeheads.

I once told Sam how pathetic you are in the dating department. It's really sad that, with all your inflated salary and bonuses, you can't even rent a date – of either sex. Why is that? Because nobody wants you, your crap personality, your overpriced condo or your fancyass sports car.

I left you there, passed out flat on your plastered face, packed my stuff and called a cab to the airport. I didn't leave you a note because your stinking behavior didn't warrant one. I suspected you'd probably figure it out when you sobered up the next day.

In your e-mail, you also wrote she was worried about my "abusive actions." Now I'm wondering just what the hell you'd told her. That I'm a violent guy on the verge of becoming a serial killer? What else did you make up, you pathological liar? Because I promise you this, worm: if I should never hear from Sam again, you'll wind up cursing Mama for ever giving birth to you.

P.

35.

When I read Pete's email to Damir, I was shell-shocked. What was with these brothers? On the surface, Damir appeared to want Pete and me to get together, but after declaring his affections for me and possibly lying about the punch to the face, I didn't know what or who to believe. This situation was fast becoming a three-ring circus. Pete was at Damir's throat, and I was the one who felt choked.

Dear Pete and Damir,

I don't want to say it, but what the hell is going on? I'm so upset I want to hide out in Alaska. Pete, I thought I knew you as a considerate, kind friend. Damir, you are a successful computer genius. Suddenly, you get together and it's World War III. No wonder you live on opposite sides of the continent.
Damir, you said Pete punched you and now Pete says you got drunk, slipped and passed out. I wonder. What *really* happened?
I'm all for letting bygones be bygones, but when you act like mercenary wannabes, I pull the emergency cord and get off the bus. You two need to sort this out. Personally, I don't believe in family counseling, but how about calling a ceasefire and having a relatively calm conversation and trying to find a solution?
I would never want to come between you, but I'm not sure if anything I did was to blame. Was I too flirty? Did I play one of you against the other unintentionally?
What has caused this insanity?

Sam

36.

Pete, you slime ball of a liar!

    You know perfectly well you took a swing at me. It doesn't make a difference that I fell and passed out. The intent was there. And what else did you tell Sam? Exactly what you said to me in your last e-mail? Is that your story?

    Because of your anger issues, she's ready to abandon ship and would rather sit in an igloo than talk to us. There you go ruining it for other people. Because you opened your big mouth, she doesn't trust either you or me and thinks the Petrovich brothers are crazy. Way to go, Woody Woodpecker.

    I never said you were a serial killer, but if the shoe fits, wear it. I confess I have feelings for Damsel Samantha and I'm throwing down the gauntlet. Encouraging you to pursue her was my way of teasing you because you don't know how to attract the right type of woman. You are so out of Sam's league. You're too old and stoic to win over a girl like her.

    I might even make the drive up to Vancouver in my Ferrari, which she LOVED when she saw it. Read 'em and weep, loser.

    By the way, I tried to sign you up for Anger Anonymous. Sadly, they don't take pit bulls.

The Better Choice
(over you, fathead)

    I punched the key to send it and took a long swallow from a beer bottle. I wiped the sweat off my brow as I sat in the hot sun on the patio with my laptop on my knees.

    I loved a good challenge and this was a fight to the finish. Chuckling to myself, I pictured Pete reaching the boiling point after my latest e-mail. I love to get under his skin whenever I can.

    Samantha is one helluva fox, but this genius is cleverer than both of them.

37.

Hey, Computer Wizard, Master Conniver & Queen of Idiot Savants Everywhere ~

Do you never tire of being a world-class asshole?

You talk about *intent*? It was pretty clear to anyone within earshot at the diner what your "intent" with Sam really was, and it was downright laughable – and sad – how you kept stepping all over your own flapping tongue. From the start, my intentions with her have always been honorable, a concept you've had much difficulty understanding throughout your shorter, loosely educated life.

If, on the off-chance that Samantha should prefer you over me, then she'll have lost my respect due to a lack of judgment and taste. So I dare you to drive to Vancouver in your precious Ferrari. Sam will send me the news clippings after tough Mama Chu deals with an unwanted interloper like you.

Consider this advance warning that I will *not* be attending your untimely funeral.

Pyotr the Invincible (also known as Peter the Great)

38.

Damir: WTF?

\#

Damir: Why haven't you texted me back, you big jerk?

\#

Damir: Your silence is getting old real fast, bro...

\#

Damir: ANSWER ME, YOU GODDAMN WEINER! NOW!!!

39.

Pete,

    Hello. Are you out there? I haven't heard from you for six weeks. I don't know if I should be sad or angry. Did you get hit by the A train and you can't contact me because you're laid up in a hospital? Or are you simply ignoring me?

    What did I do to put you off? Are you mad because I called you a mercenary? Or because I said I wanted to escape to Alaska? Tears are rolling down my face. Not hearing from you is worse than even an angry response. At least let me know you're alive. I can't stand this. Please call me or write me something, anything at all.

Remember me?
Sam

40.

Finalizing my plans after the Oakland "vacation" took more than a month's time, almost the rest of the summer, in fact. My reason not to contact Samantha or my underhanded brother in any way was to prevent tipping my hand, extremely critical to my success. The first thing a good poker player learns is how to keep his cards close to his chest.

It was tricky business, but everything's a done deal. People can be royally pissed off with me and call me any foul names they want, but no one alive can ever claim that Peter Sergei Petrovich has never been a man of action. Why? Simply because I've just proven every one of them liars.

The time was at hand to drop a long overdue e-mail into Sam's inbox...

Subject: How's Your Radar Working, Psychic One?

Dear Sam ~

You have my sincerest apologies for the lack of any contact or response from yours truly of late. The last thing I ever wanted was to make you feel sad, so dry those eyes because in mere seconds you will know precisely my reasons why.

I've unpacked most of the many boxes of clothes, books and stereo equipment at my new place. Compared to Greenwich Village and other parts of my former city, this is a reasonably-priced unit. It's modern, clean and bright with everything I need. Great view of a tree-lined street and a small park nearby. The people here are friendly, not rushing to be somewhere else. (The morons given to big sales in NY are attracted by ads that read "Doorbusters.")

So why did I do all this?

First, I got fed up with NYC. Second, I was sick of my job. Third, I needed to be closer to you. Much closer, and in more ways than the obvious one. It was the biggest risk of my whole life, especially if you should suddenly happen to assume that I'm one of those stalker guys.

My bosses were constantly on my back to the point I was developing a serious stomach ulcer. So I quit my job with sufficient notice, left the city and state and moved to...Vancouver. I have a job downtown and I'm only about a mile from you. I am pleased to be able to change the spelling of the word "neighbor" to "neighbour." The new address and landline are attached.

I understand your classes will be resuming shortly and I won't try to mess up your schedule. Before then, I'll try to answer any and all questions you may have, but not until I ask you for our first official date this coming weekend. (Lunch in San Francisco didn't count.) What would you like to do on either Friday or Saturday night? Catch a movie? Take a walk in Vancouver Park? If a ship or canoe can be had, how about a moonlight cruise off the waters of your scenic shoreline? You say it. We'll do it. Thanks.

Love,
Petya

41.

I was stunned to learn Peter was in Vancouver. And he moved here on my account? Could this really be true? All of my anger and apprehension melted away like ice in the summer sun, replaced by the fire's glow of inner warmth. Despite a few of Pete's temper outbursts, he had proven he truly cared about me.

The family feud between Pete and Damir probably started at a young age. My sixth sense told me his wrath toward Damir was based on jealousy between competing brothers. I didn't need to be afraid of Pete as his intentions were nothing but honorable. My own feelings of anger were not so unlike his; we just expressed them differently. Pete felt things deeply. I'd seen his different sides, but his heart was in the right place.

42.

I've had an itch that I can't scratch since the big blow-out, but winning that productivity bonus provided me another two-week vacation with pay. My mechanic just got the Ferrari tuned up perfectly. As the car and I are both in rare form, I'm thinking it's time that I make a fast run to Canada to see if sexy Sam can help with this persistent itch of mine.

Dearest Sam,

Great news, sweetie. I was awarded more vacation time for a recent achievement of mine and would like to spend it all with you in Vancouver. What I need ASAP is your home address and road directions there. I can't wait to see you again! Thanks!

Damir

P.S.: You and I are gonna party hardy!!!

43.

I thought I'd have a major panic attack on my first day on the new job, but for starters, the gentle breeze outside my apartment was refreshingly brisk while something elusive on the way to work hinted that I should not be overly concerned. Something in the air seemed to be missing – and it was the constant blaring of car horns during the morning rush hour. Ah, true civilization, the way it should truly be.

My boss greeted me warmly with a smile and a firm handshake as we had an impromptu conference upon my arrival. What a difference from my last two supervisors. And then an even bigger surprise as he showed me to an office instead of a cold, nondescript work cubicle.

* * *

Tuesday: It's been a huge relief (no pun intended) to be able to use the restroom without being stalked by anyone as sex-crazed as "Lucy in the Sky with Dagger Eyes."

Wednesday: My new office comrades took me to lunch at a nearby upscale restaurant. When it came time to pay the tab, I reached for my wallet to cover my portion of that delicious seafood meal, but my attempt was soundly thwarted in unison by these friendly and generous Vancouverite co-workers. "Don't worry," one said on the way out, "you'll have a chance to pay it forward soon enough when the next hire signs on."

Thursday: I was complimented in writing to my supervisor by two pleased clients. Those "atta boys" always help to reinforce the hiring staff's insightful decisions.

TGIF – and payday.

But the best surprise of the entire week was when I received a call from Sam.

"Hey, Pete, congratulations for getting through your first week. Many kudos and props to you for that."

"Thanks. It went far better than I could have imagined, but I must say it's an equally great feeling to hear your lovely, sweet voice speaking into my lonely ear right now."

"So, I'm in the mood to celebrate tonight. How about you? Up for it?"

"Anything special in mind?"

"To begin with, dinner for two at a swanky restaurant would be damned appropriate."

I paused. "Not some greasy diner like the one Damir took us to in San Francisco?"

She laughed. "No way. Not even close, I promise."

"Then I accept your most kind invite without reservation."

"Ah, but I will be the one to make a reservation for us. And who knows might happen later?"

44.

Prior to my dinner date later that evening with Peter, I felt I had to send one final email before I eventually became deluged with any additional love notes from his slightly deranged and terminally infatuated kid brother...

Hello Damir,

I received your email, but I think it's better that you don't come to see me. To put it bluntly, I'm turning you down.

Did you have any inkling that Peter moved here? Well, he has. I couldn't believe it at first.

I was angry before when he didn't write. I was afraid he'd dropped out of the grid to live in South America or somewhere, but when we finally did connect, I was so relieved to know he was alive and well. When he wrote that he'd moved to Vancouver, I was so surprised I spilled half a cup of coffee onto my laptop. However, I haven't been on the computer lately because Pete and I have started spending a lot of time together. Dating him is more than I could have imagined.

Also I wanted to say even though Pete and you have had bad blood in the past, I hope one day you two can put it behind you. Life is too short. Stay well and spend that vacation time in Oakland with some nice girls. You need to get out more.

Take care for now.

Best wishes,
Samantha

45.

WTF? That no-good sonuvabitch has gotten to the finish line first? Before *me* – the heartthrob of Samantha's passionate desires? That no-good, low-down sneaky bastard! Put it behind me? Life is too short? What kind of rhetoric is that? This isn't over.

How the hell am I ever going to wrest his paws off of that gorgeous babe *now*?

46.

Pete and I sat on the family's front porch swing on a warm and waning September eve as we held hands and enjoyed ice-cold bottles of Kokanee. If I'd thought his moving here had been a bombshell, my poker-playing "James Dean" had one left to top it by a country mile.

"If I hadn't been granted a work visa, I would've been forced to alter my plans by staying in the U.S. and moving to one of the northernmost cities in Washington State – Birch Bay, Blaine or Lynden – and commuting across the border to keep on seeing you as much as possible."

"Really? You would have done that?"

"You bet. But it was also difficult finding a trucking outfit to haul up here what little furniture and clothes I own, along with the best of my books, music and movies. That was a nightmare. In fact, they had to transfer all the contents in Washington for a Canadian freight company that could deliver the goods to my new address in British Columbia.

"And there were several things I made sure to do before I left New York. One was to leave behind a small, significant item for Miss Lucy, something I hid in her desk drawer. How I would've loved to be that proverbial fly on the wall to see her shocked and scandalized face when, in full view of her male peers, she slowly opened the..."

"You didn't? A sex toy?"

I laughed again, although this time it was more of an evil schoolyard snicker.

"Not quite."

"So tell me. What was it?"

"Okay. It was a pair of small mechanical monkeys. When you flip the switch, they go at it hot and heavy. And what a racket they make. Trust me, she deserved it. Oh, did she ever..."

"You are such a bad boy sometimes."

We took a moment to sip some more ale.

"Another must-do item. It's become a recent fun trend there, but a huge annoyance to our city officials and frustrated sanitation workers."

"What kind of trendy thing?"

"It has to do with locks."

"Ah, like locks of hair?"

Peter laughed. "No, more like small, metal locks for bicycles and the combination type for school lockers."

I was puzzled. "What in heaven's name could be trendy about things like them?"

"People involved with this deal, especially lovers, paint on their names or initials and then attach 'em to the pedestrian walkway railings of the many bridges over the Hudson and East Rivers. I just had to leave one prominently displayed, playfully swaying in the constant breezes."

"And you put your name on it?"

"Nope. Initials. Ours – S&P. They also stand for a last-minute reminder of Wall Street's good ol' financial barometer, Standard & Poor's."

"And you say you're not creative."

"What *is* creative is all the nonstop cussin' being done by sanitation workers having to saw them off as they constantly plead on the news for us to knock off this vandal-like stuff. They have had to remove them by the hundreds. Maybe thousands. Bridge cables are now sagging and straining under the combined weight of all those little and otherwise innocuous metal locks."

I shook my head as I wondered how crazy New Yorkers could be, but decided not to offer an opinion. Instead I posed Pete a question. "Anything else you needed to do?"

"Yeah, the other was to have lunch with Anne Leroy. After reading the sample chapter, she requested the full manuscript and fell in love with it. Her biggest problem is that she doesn't act as an agent for anyone outside the States."

As he paused with brow furrowed and a deep frown, I feared the demise of any future success of my novel. I must have gone pale because Peter was unable to keep a straight face for very long.

"What?" I grabbed his arm and shook it. "You're holding something back. Tell me!"

"Well, I guess you can handle it. Anne has a partner in Seattle who handles writers outside of the United States. Her name is Laura Edison and she'll be contacting you to offer a contract to be your literary agent. And Anne assured me the book will not take long to find a publisher..."

I roared and hugged Pete until he could barely breathe.

"Quiet," he said, choking and gasping for air. "Do you want Mama Chu to think I'm out here attacking you?"

"You really *are* Peter the Great."

"Nah, not really," he said with his usual modesty, the colour gradually returning to his face, "but there's something I must ask. What's your next writing project?"

"It's already begun."

"Then it's your turn now to tell *me*," said a surprised Pete. "What's it about?"

"I don't have a final title yet, but for now, the working one is *US*."

"*US*?"

"Yep. It stands for *Untitled Story*, but mainly because it's all about *us*..."

Legacy

By James D. Young

"Hopper is simply a bad painter, but if he were a better one, he would probably not be such a great artist."
– Clement Greenberg

On a bitterly cold morning in early March, one which had Benjamin Englander home sick again from high school, the doorbell rang. Putting on a robe, he took his time getting to the front of his parents' house. He opened the door and bent down to pick up the new telephone books left there. Carrying them into the den and setting them on the credenza near the phone, he noticed the picture gracing the cover of the 1971 residential White Pages. It revealed a deserted city street in muted colors from a bygone era.

After dinner, he showed the cover to his father. Glancing up from the paper, he asked, "Norman Rockwell? Perhaps reprinted from an old issue of *The Saturday Evening Post*?"

"I thought so, too, at first," Benjamin said. "Very similar in content, but it seems so much more desolate. There's none of Rockwell's warmth or subtle humor or –"

"Inside they indicate the title is 'Early Sunday Morning.' Looks much like a 1920s or '30s street scene from an old jigsaw puzzle of Rockwell's my father once put together. He did it on a homemade wooden board, I might add. 1,000 pieces, it was. Your late grandpapa was crafty. Very good with wood."

"This artist's name is Edward Hopper."

"You know, son, I think I've heard that name before. School of Realism or some such. Believe the man might have passed on a few years ago."

"I...I like it. With your permission, I'd like to save the cover when the year is done."

His father laughed. "Always thinking ahead, aren't you, Ben? I wish you'd give that kind of foresight to your future. You do graduate next June. But, yes, you may have it."

A good son, but Ben was considered nerdy by his classmates long before that pejorative adjective came into being. A loner almost cast in the mold of Salinger's Holden Caulfield, but without possessing that character's rebellious nature and outspokenness, he had far more in common with inveterate daydreamer Walter Mitty. Frail and prone to illness, shy and socially awkward, the boy compensated by working diligently in school, but drove counselors – and his parents – batty by drifting away from setting any cast-in-stone goals for his life.

Just before winter break, one of his teachers had shown the class a 16mm print of *On the Waterfront* for a special after-school occasion. Despite being released almost two decades earlier, it was Ben's first brush with realism. He was riveted by the power of a story which had retained the in-close portrayal of life in the gritty world of the Hoboken piers over the years.

He knew he could never have the strength and dogged determination of Terry Malloy, but he admired those qualities just the same. Conversely, he was deeply touched by that character's conflicted love interest, the vulnerability and girlish innocence of Edie Doyle. Exposed to this rough world of hardened people seduced by corruption and greed, he was unaware that he was birthing an eye for realism as well as for stark beauty.

In high school art classes, Ben was able to appreciate works of Klee, Kandinsky and Miró, but did not understand them any more than he did the erratic paint drippings of Jackson Pollock. French artists such as Monet, Gauguin and Cézanne did not affect him in any way. He felt Van Gogh's "Starry, Starry Night" was the result of some kind of vision-inducing narcotic available to him by apothecaries of his day. But Hopper's work spoke to him; no, those paintings cried out to him and invited him within, deeper, to explore the moments surrounding whatever actions were depicted by the artist.

He spotted an advertisement for an Edward Hopper exhibition at the Whitney scheduled to begin September 10th. Without benefit of a girlfriend, Ben chose instead to take his 10-year-old cousin into the city for it the next day. She ooh'd and aah'd at the colors and size of Hopper's paintings, but years later, she would be unable to recall a single thing about the event.

Standing in front of Hopper's massive "Railroad Sunset," Ben was in awe. Steel rails glimmered, unused at that moment in time. To the left was the decrepit signal tower. Ben imagined stepping into this scene, climbing up the rickety staircase and speaking with the towerman there. Throughout the afternoon, he returned to view this painting no fewer than a dozen times.

Before he considered purchasing the souvenir booklet, printed on quality art stock, he ensured that "Railroad Sunset" was included. It was, and as stunning in its greatly reduced size as the original from which he could not stay away.

Weeks later, he clipped a Sunday newspaper reproduction, but the colors were washed. The one in his booklet was superior by far. Along with several postcards of the man's etchings and oils, he felt as if he had added immeasurably to his worldly treasures, but the hefty price of the Abrams' coffee table tome by Lloyd Goodrich remained far beyond his means. It would have to wait until he had a steady job, and a well-paying one at that.

As deeply autistic children will perseverate at various repetitive tasks, and always to the point of obsession, so it took hold of Ben's life as he immediately began devoting two days each month to visit the New York Public Library at 42nd and Fifth, "Crossroads of the World" he had often heard it called. He jotted capsule impressions in his notebook of Hopper's oils and etchings as he studied each from books literally for hours:

Sept. 14: "Chop Suey" (1929) – Reminds me of downtown. Mother's stories when she and father were courting in the '40s told of frequenting inexpensive restaurants such as this. By then, cloche hats for flapper ladies as these two are wearing here were no longer in fashion. Is the man in the background with his wife? Or his mistress? He seems so formal and rigid, almost aloof. And the dining room is two or three stories above street level.

Sept. 27: "Rooms for Tourists" (1945) – Deceptive night scene awaiting a scary short story by Ray Bradbury or a creepy "Night Gallery" episode.

Oct. 9: "Approaching a City" (1946) – Sooty residue from the smokestacks of passing steam locomotives is visible on the grime-coated concrete portal overhead. A most dreary view.

Oct. 30: "House by the Railroad" (1925) – No doubt Alfred Hitchcock had seen this one. How else could he have imagined the Bates mansion? Perfect timing for Halloween.

Nov. 15: "The Circle Theatre" (1935) – Found in only one book so far. Traffic lights were red and green. No middle amber warning. But what movie was showing? Why did Hopper place an old subway kiosk at dead center, thereby obscuring the neon lighted art-deco marquee???

Dec. 20: "Nighthawks" (1942) – Has to be one of the man's masterpieces! I believe I'd enjoy drinking coffee alongside these people and eavesdropping on their secretive conversations.

Regardless of whether Hopper's works were in color or black and white, they seemed to draw Ben to them at first, and then into the actual scenes themselves, populated or not. He began to daydream about the various and almost endless possibilities of what had just occurred or would happen shortly thereafter. His Mitty-like imagination was set aflame.

After graduation, he had hand-delivered his application to Brooklyn's prestigious Pratt Institute, but it was rejected. Years earlier, his pencil and crayon doodlings of houses, trees, dogs and cats from matchbook covers ("Draw me!") never garnered any sales pitches from the Famous Artists outfit in Connecticut. Not even a patronizing reply. He'd always assumed the envelopes had been lost in transit and not that his childish attempts were poor and unpromising.

During this time of unabated unemployment, he received a letter of acceptance from a small school devoted to the visual arts located in a seedy section of lower Manhattan. He convinced his father to convert their one-car garage into a studio with a skylight. The price was far more than his parents could comfortably afford, but they acquiesced out of a potential hope for any future successes he may have. Resigned to moving the battered but utilitarian Volkswagen twice a week for the city's alternate-side-of-the-street parking requirements, his father received but one ticket.

Ben's art was abysmal. Nothing he produced remotely ignited trails blazed by Hopper. Not in technique, not in touch. Whether he used pen and ink, pastels, watercolors or oils on canvas, nothing ever gelled. And, frustrated, he knew it. There was no hope. No future. He became depressed that his parents had expended so much capital on a doomed-from-the-start venture. Stillborn.

The following spring, Ben began noticing especially clear days not recognized in any of his younger years. The way the sun lit storefronts and created sharply delineated degrees of shadows on sidewalks made him think of Hopper's art.

On this day, he ran home for his old point-and-shoot Kodak Instamatic. Loading a roll of film, he revisited this commonplace street and snapped a number of shots, carefully watching the counter as the film advanced. The green and red metal of the candy store's Coca-Cola sign overhead had new life breathed into it. Broken chunks of old macadam revealed Belgian cobblestones and steel trolley tracks never removed, just paved over. And there was something odd in the atmosphere that was registering differently with him. Having just read Toffler's *Future Shock*, a thought occurred, compelling him to preserve all this before it was too soon gone: "I must do this!"

One month later, he accompanied his parents to a wedding in Denville, New Jersey, on a similarly clear weather morning. His camera always with him now, he felt a shiver as he detrained and observed the rear Erie Lackawanna car. As it slowly left the station for Dover, its large rear light glowing bright red, he snapped a shot on the run. With no time to compose it properly, yet without seeing a finished print – and wouldn't for a week – he knew it would turn out to be a subject worthy of a Hopper painting. And it did.

Ben's father was extremely encouraging, but his mother could hardly be considered supportive regarding this hobby of his. Somewhat prudish, she was uneasy with art books containing unclad people and voiced her concerns to her husband. Ben overheard a conversation to that effect drifting from their bedroom one night. Said his father in a rare tone of annoyance, "They're only models, for God's sake. Artists have always used them for the study of anatomy. Would you prefer Benjamin patronize those sleazy dens of porn in Times Square for his?"

There was no audible reply, and he never heard his mother bring up the subject again.

The rationale behind Hopper's nudes eluded Ben, and so he eschewed any for his own use. He found them rather mundane and almost sad, without the air-brushed erotic perfection of females found within the pages of *Playboy*. "Evening Wind" was an etching he liked, not because the woman kneeling on the bed was nude, but because of the soft billowing motion of the sheer window curtain. To him, that and her imagined desires were the catalysts creating the electricity-charged atmosphere in her lonely room.

Once, in summer, and when no one was home, he undressed and walked through each room of the house. He felt awkward, especially near windows, and found sitting on plastic-covered or leather furniture, even fabric, felt sticky or scratchy. Decidedly uncomfortable. He retrieved his clothes, dressed, and did not engage in any like experiments again.

By December, however, any people unfortunate to be traveling outdoors were chilled down to the bone by Canadian-originating cold fronts. Yet in rapidly diminishing twilight, Ben braved this wicked weather and a persistent runny nose to take a ground-level photograph of the signal mechanism located on the elevated train structure above. To the right was a lone, leafless skeleton of a tree bough encroaching near the side of the el's metal railing. He took only one shot.

When Ben's print was developed at the local drugstore the following week, the deep green of that signal's lens, as well as the dormant tree and gradation of the sky's light from dark blue to magenta, conveyed the numbing cold he'd experienced when capturing that moment.

Something created by nature occurred overnight as 1973 dawned, something freakish that Ben had never known to exist or could ever anticipate – an ice storm. The decaying neighborhood was transformed into an awe-inspiring wonderland, but hardly a safe one as overhead power lines snapped under the weight of frozen rain and whipped around on the ground with lively showers of sparks. Touching them would be fatal, Con Edison crews advised residents.

From material Ben had on hand, he could not recall any Hopper painting that contained snow or ice as its subject, but concluded he would have if he had been exposed to vistas such as these. Ben worked the camera's shutter as he strode and slipped through the silent ice-covered morning.

Shortly after the peace accords were signed in Paris near month's end and the long war finally over, a parcel of foreign origin arrived. Excited, Ben knew exactly what the box contained. A neighbor, serving in the Air Force and who had flown a number of missions in Vietnam, kept his promise and had mailed him a

35mm Minolta Single Lens Reflex camera directly from the Philippines at Ben's own earlier holiday request. Import duty fees included, the total price was less than half the cost of its stateside counterpart. He could never have afforded it otherwise.

Ben immediately fell in love with this sleek SLR. It molded to his hand as if he were born with it, its weight and balance part of him. He never reverted to his Kodak, nor did he ever purchase another model, save for various lenses and filters.

By April, Ben had learned most of the Minolta's intricacies and felt like a consummate professional, photographing the newly-built and open-for-business World Trade Center located in lower Manhattan. As he lay on his back on the busy sidewalk to capture the twin towers joining upward into an almost single pinnacle, he laughed when he heard a businessman say while stepping over him, "Sober up and get a job, ya bum."

He spotted and photographed a smiling John Lennon that June in a Central Park meadow. Ben's later "Dakota" photograph found itself in great demand. Shadows played and mixed with odd sunlight on and near the distinctive Gothic apartments, with the contrasting foliage of the park as background. In light of the beloved singer's later assassination there, it took on an overtly eerie quality as well.

His father, understanding how that year's recession was affecting many job applicants, including his son, sat down with him and made an intriguing business proposal.

"If I were to assist you with seed money, would you consider printing some of your photos to adorn postcards, stationery, note cards and the like? If you have some success, you can repay the loan as you earn."

Ben promised that he would think it over and accepted the proposal by the end of the week with a handshake, a gentlemen's agreement between father and son.

Despite limited income from a part-time job as a grocery bagger and cashier at a King Kullen in Ozone Park, Ben finally decided, with father's financial help, to enlarge and frame some of his better efforts. He'd submitted several to magazines, but every one was summarily rejected. To offset any residual negativity, he arranged to display his work in Greenwich Village during the art show and was surprised to find that many sold, and at unexpected prices. As a newcomer, he priced no glass-and-chrome framed photograph higher than thirty-five dollars, yet they sold as fast as he could display fresh prints.

A man kept returning to eye the train signal photo, the one Ben had taken at dusk last winter and dubbed "El Sentinel." Removing a business card from his pocket, he handed it to Ben. It was for a relatively new magazine which extolled the joys of life in New York City. The man said, "I'm the assistant editor and I'd like very much for you to bring that one right there to my office next Monday morning as I believe it's exactly what I want – and need – to illustrate an upcoming feature article. God, its stark, realistic beauty gives me chills. We can discuss payment and rights for its use then. Please call me, won't you?"

The editor reached out and shook his hand with enthusiasm. Ben wasn't exactly sure how to feel, but he could hardly deny that it wasn't a great sensation.

"A magazine editor had just liked my work? Pinch me hard, someone. I think I'm dreaming again..."

Ben began taking courses in developing negatives and producing both monochromatic and color prints. The one-car garage was converted this time into a darkroom. Included now was plumbing for a sink, almost as costly as before. Ben's output was increasing, as was his acceptance within the local art community. He never had to perform special tricks to get his photographs to stand out as well as they did. Their artistic draw was intrinsic.

One entry titled "Couple Waiting for a Train" was shot through a Lackawanna train window in strong noon sunlight at the Newark Broad Street station. Sitting on the wood bench was a young couple. The woman, head and eyes downcast, gave off a feeling of despair – did she just learn she was pregnant? Her presumed boyfriend, emotionally detached, looked westward for an approaching train. Shadows filtering through the wrought-iron fencing made fresh, exaggerated designs on the ground and created a uniquely new hue for the station's red brick, in stark contrast to existing urban blight on the horizon. If one could break a dimensional wall, step into this scene and speak, the pervasive silence of this captured moment would be irrevocably shattered.

"Redbirds" had a lone man looking disheveled and leaning

Legacy

against a defunct penny gum machine as a red IRT train entered a Bronx el station, while "9th Hole," taken one month later, became another prized shot taken from a slow-moving commuter train as it passed an unpopulated and unused section of a municipal golf course. The blue flag waved in the stiff wind while autumn leaves swirled around the manicured green, now flecked with brown.

These were followed the next winter by the Manhattan/Brooklyn Bridge snowfall series, each one dreamily serene. And as spring arrived, "Barber Shop" was just that – two old Toledo-style chairs, vacant, with the proprietor idly reading a magazine near the front pane-glass window.

Ben's awareness of photographers, experienced and new, began to grow – Berenice Abbott and her public works-sponsored New York cityscapes during the Great Depression, Ansel Adams for his majestic mountain ranges and Annie Leibovitz for her rock star portraits. Others emerged over time, such as David Plowden, but Ben remained unconcerned about any competition or conflicts. He didn't feel talented enough to run with these big dogs.

Several women gathered around a stark black-and-white grouping of four prints at Ben Englander's first gallery exhibition. "Telly's" revealed a simple Greek snack bar which did business near a private pool in the mid-1970s. The outside of the diminutive wooden building, photographed in a gentle way from a side angle, was idyllically shaded by large leafy trees. Charmed, one could immediately feel drawn to it. Inside, with an antique metal cash register in the foreground, a weary waitress handed a tow-headed boy an ice cream cone. His expression seemed pleased, not just for the summer treat, but because he was receiving change as well.

Framed lengthwise as a window would be, the third photo featured a light cloth shade with an embroidered pull-ring. The last was a side shot of Telly himself as he washed dishes. What made it memorable was a black letterboard to his right which listed menu prices, frozen now in time, never to be victims of the ravages of inflation.

One woman questioned if the café's owner might be related to another famous Greek, the current star of television's popular "Kojak" series, or if that Telly might be the actual owner. Passing by, Ben overheard her question and said to her, "You might have something there, ma'am. And, you know, it never even crossed my mind to ask."

When they stopped laughing, they lavishly praised him for his talents. His face began to redden, and he stammered a "Thank you kindly" as he headed to the far wall.

Another group of mixed older individuals stood transfixed in front of "Fog." A young woman's face – he'd used a friend from the neighborhood – stared with cold eyes into the camera's lens. Shrouded in thick night mist, only one side of her face was revealed, similar to the "Meet the Beatles" album cover. Behind her were the colors of distant traffic signals, every one out of focus. The effect was hypnotic.

By evening's end, the consensus leaned heavily toward Ben's "Park Breakfast" as a preview of masterpieces yet to be created. By itself, it was simply a gorgeous framing of a pristine snowfall in Washington Square Park, until he introduced a warm touch of humanity by focusing on an old man, coffee cup in hand, and feeding tiny pieces of a stale roll and bagel with the other to a gathering of birds.

Some critics were quite taken with his gallery debut, this limited oeuvre, while others took a more conservative wait-and-see attitude. A noted critic, the prissy and often acerbic Thomas La Plante, was hardly effusive in his review, but managed to find a few words of encouragement:

"As this youngster does display a modicum of budding talent, it is my fervent wish that he is never tempted nor lured by fleeting illusions of money and fame."

None, however, could see as yet the subtle parallels bridging the world of Hopper's old art with Englander's new photography. Still, there was no denying his gradual and eventual success: three books continuously in print, each a greater best-seller than its predecessor. Sales of his signed, limited editions continued to increase, as did exhibitions and appearances, although Ben dreaded talk shows, radio or television. That shy streak was always a tough one for him to beat, but he was most decidedly on his way.

After scouting several lush adjoining properties in Branford, a stone's throw east of downtown New Haven, he convinced his parents to put their house on the market so that they could remain close. The moving van completed the daunting task in the summer of 1985, and Ben turned his photographic attention to the small water craft docked in various marinas or to the yawls gliding on rivers of glass. He also kept his sharp eye peeled for New England lighthouses. Always.

Later photographs created during excursions to New York environs captured a comely woman sitting self-consciously on a rattan seat aboard a vintage elevated transit car, Coney Island's famous Wonder Wheel evident in the background. Its underground counterpart, the color-faded "Subway Newsstand" featured a middle-aged man of indeterminate ethnicity with no Sunday customers. His head canted at an angle and with eyes focused on the ground, this swarthy fellow's moment of utter loneliness and boredom became a drab Hopperesque one.

These two were followed by "Kites" – two children, faces obscured in shade, flying them in the distance atop the wheat-colored hill of a park.

Over on Staten Island, he found an anachronistic black 1949 Packard sitting silent and alone, covered in dust on the floor of a car dealership's showroom. He titled the print after the vehicle.

"Admission" was in soft focus outside a cold, nondescript concrete stadium. It captured a solitary man in a camel's hair overcoat as he was purchasing a ticket for a college football game from an agent, out of sight behind the window.

One of his most disquieting images was the black-and-white "Girl in Summer." Taken on a Long Island beach, it revealed a young woman in a dress as she sat, lost in thought, on a folding wooden chair in the soft gray sand. Behind her rose a smooth dune untouched by human feet. Wind blew through her blonde tresses, and the photograph came to life, breathing lightly with the spirit of Edward Hopper.

Success does not come without a price, and the cost for Ben Englander in 1992 was the onset of Albers-Schonberg disease, commonly known as osteoporosis, coupled shortly afterward with a second diagnosis, that of the crippling effects of hypertrophic arthritis. The doctors played their which-came-first game – the chicken or the egg? It didn't really matter. He had acquired both. And he accepted both. These diseases would certainly curtail his photographic activities in time, but for now he could navigate without the assistance of crutches on most days. The use of a wheelchair would not be required for a while.

Ben's parents tended to him frequently, their hearts breaking, but both remained stoic in his presence. Not only did they love the home he had provided for them, but they also loved him so much more because of how selflessly he'd achieved the move with them seven years before.

In the spring of 1997, members of the Symposium of Art and Photography would hardly allow a quarter-century of Ben's work to pass without notice. They decided May would be a perfect time to bestow upon him their Eye of the Beholder Award for a lifetime of superior achievements. They'd known, from rare interviews given, he had always indicated that spring date when he'd bolted home to retrieve his Kodak so that he could shoot street scenes in his former Brooklyn neighborhood.

On Saturday evening of the Memorial Day weekend, patrons of the arts, Ben's peers, fans, friends and well-wishers filled the main hall of Lincoln Center in tribute. A retrospective slide show of his photographs was projected overhead on a continuous basis, accompanied by the evocative, haunting melodies of Pachelbel's "Canon in D" and Chopin's "Fantasie-Impromptu, Op. 66," among several other timeless classics.

After a stirring, heartfelt introduction by the Symposium president, Benjamin Englander hobbled across the stage with the assistance of aluminum hand-held wrist crutches. He paused in front of the podium's microphone, wiped something from the corner of his eye and smiled at his parents in the first row while quietly clearing his throat.

"Distinguished members, mother, father, and all my dearest friends, if you were to assume that a lifelong case of shyness would disappear from my life at this point, you'd be…so very wrong."

Laughter and love filled the hall.

"Thank you very much for being here and for those kind words already said. It seems everything I've achieved I owe first and foremost to a Power far greater than mere mortals, and also to one man in particular, a most talented man, who passed on before I graduated from elementary school. The renowned artist Edward Hopper died before I knew the man even existed.

"It has been proven to me time and again that death does not end a life. Death does not cut short one's ability to influence. Death does not rob us of works of art, be they music, literature, paintings or photography, created and left to us by others more skilled and talented than we. Death cannot usurp the beauty of the world's treasures, legacies so richly needed by the human race.

"I must admit to you that it was never my intent to imitate or, even worse, to copy Hopper's distinctive style. What I believe did happen is that, through some ironic twist or intervention of fate, I developed a strange and inexplicable ability to view this city and the world through the eyes of a deceased artist. Edward Hopper was showing me his world, but did so from the great beyond. In that way, he…was guiding…me."

His voice lowered. "If not for that, I have no other suitable explanation."

The sound of silence within the hall was deafening.

"To all of you here tonight, to you who have so honored me this evening, I make one promise and will do my utmost to keep it: I shall continue in my chosen field, my life's work, as long as I am physically able. If I can retain the ability to open an eyelid, to be able to focus, if I can depress a shutter with a prosthetic hand or finger, then so be it."

His parents wept. A standing ovation with thunderous applause echoed in Ben's ears. Despite the pain, despite the knowledge that his condition would continue to degenerate, effectively putting an end to his creative days, this moment provided him with the finest healing medicine one could hope to obtain, and at any price.

During the final summer of his life, wheelchair-bound Ben spoke to his now-elderly parents about a daytrip he wished to complete on his own. He would hire a car and revisit some of the locales he'd lovingly photographed during the last quarter-century.

The car arrived early Sunday morning. Caleb the driver introduced himself and assisted the handicapped man into a comfortable position upon the limousine's spacious rear seat. He placed a blanket near Ben in case the weather should grow cooler by evening.

"Would you care to take your Minolta along with you, Benjamin?" his mother asked.

"It's already in my coat pocket," he said, blowing her a kiss and waving to his father.

Traffic was unusually light on the turnpike from Branford straight to the Bronx. They made their first stop in Queens. Ben searched for landmarks, only to find that the private pool was gone, filled in and replaced by an automotive front end, brakes and body shop. Telly's, next door to the right and later converted to a South American fast-food place, had been gutted by a fire.

They drove to Brooklyn and to the el. Although the tree had long been reduced to firewood, the elevated structure was standing, rusty and neglected, but more or less intact and operational. Staring up at the lone signal perched high above, he noted its number and swore it was the same one. Pleased, Ben grinned. It represented his breakthrough photo.

His smile soon faded and his heart grew heavy when he learned from a longtime resident his subject of the mesmerizing, award-winning "Fog" photo had been severely beaten in a street fight several years before. She'd died in a hospital days afterward.

They drove on to downtown Brooklyn, to the bridges and docks. On the waterfront streets of Washington and Water, where he had captured the majesty of the Manhattan Bridge support tower on a spring night, he found the area had festered and become a dumping ground for old sofas and other large trashed items. The sight of this site now overwhelmed and depressed him.

At the borough's other end an hour later, he found that Coney Island seemed to lack the spirit and attractions which had made it world famous decades earlier. Ben instructed his driver to find a parking space on Stillwell Avenue.

"Caleb, have you ever had a Nathan's hot dog?"

"Can't say that I have, Mr. Englander."

"Ah, a wasted life," he said, deadpan. "But you're plenty youthful, and it's never too late to start. Besides, I'm buying."

After lunch and lemonade, they crossed the Verrazzano-Narrows Bridge and headed to the far end of Staten Island. There, in Tottenville, overlooking the New Jersey city of Perth Amboy across the channel, Rando Auto Sales was long gone, along with its lone dusty '49 Packard.

Ben, growing bone-weary toward dusk, asked to be driven home. Contemplating thoughts from this day, he spoke very little on the return journey.

Time having moved inexorably forward, the mystery and magic of these places had disappeared. Still, he quietly thanked his version of a deity for allowing him, at the very least, the time and talent to be able to preserve a small part of them. Sleepy, he closed his eyes to rest them from the harsh and irritating glare of passing night traffic.

He recalled that few interviewers ever asked him which photograph was his favorite. One had often been overlooked, except by a single person. After the initial release of *The Exorcist*, it found its way into many a small local theater to attract more paying customers eager to be terrified. In one of the boroughs, he always forgot exactly where, he snapped a fast shot of three parochial schoolgirls in uniform under the marquee's title. They seemed nervous while fumbling for money as they approached the ticket booth and tried hard to muster the courage to attend. "Abandon Hope, Ye Who Enter" appeared in his first book.

Some years thereafter, he received a large manila envelope with no return address. It contained a black-and-white movie still, autographed by a lead cast member. She had inscribed it, "Dearest Ben, you make my head spin!" It generated the biggest – and most unexpected – laugh of his life, and he immediately had it framed. That signed photo has remained on display on his mantle over the fireplace ever since, one of his most cherished possessions.

"I'll have you back home in less than an hour. Are you comfortable back there, sir?"

"More than I can say, Caleb. Thank you for asking."

But Ben frowned as he touched the camera in his pocket. He hadn't taken a single photograph today and was forced to conclude there was nothing worth taking.

As he began slipping into a light nap, he wondered if his own legacy, like Hopper's, might stand the test of time to survive him. Would it live on for others? Who knows? Only the future has that answer, he mused, and then, lulled by the soothing, steady rhythm of the road, did he drift off into a restful, satisfying sleep.

James D. Young

* * *

A slow-paced, character-driven independent film, *Don't Come Knocking*, made its American premiere to decent reviews at the Directors Guild Theater in Manhattan on March 9, 2006. Seven years earlier, and to the very day and hour, Benjamin Englander, following his artistic mentor, had slipped quietly from this world.

Equally ironic were the many visually stunning scenes shot by cinematographer Franz Lustig in Nevada, Utah and Montana. Whether his focus was on sunlight, on angles of buildings or on the lonely, alienated people in the story, these images achieved up on the big screen what Hopper had committed to canvas and Englander to photographic paper.

And it did not go unnoticed by an actress who had appeared in the film.

Toward the end of her career, but brimming with a lifetime of perception, Eva Marie Saint said in a filmed interview, "An incredible eye! It was Edward Hopper in Butte, Montana. It was seeing through *his* eyes..."

Inner Circle

By Sandra Yuen MacKay

Chapter 1

Sean Abrams believed Vancouver, British Columbia was the best city in the world to inhabit for one reason. Despite traffic, the high cost of living and pollution, it was such a beautiful city in which to reside. Attracting tourists and people from around the world created an interesting mix of cultures. However, more than anything he lived there because he had a secret.

He rarely left town because of his job as head of a law firm. There were always new clients and new cases—not to mention repeat clients. He was clever and forthright in his work. As a lawyer, he was a bit of a sleuth, digging for information to aid his clients' cases, including investigating every lead, leaving nothing to chance in the courtroom. He had built his firm with the best lawyers he could find and now took a more senior role.

Despite the demands of his firm, these days his only daughter was forefront on his mind. Jennifer was an attractive, young woman. She worked as a legal secretary at his firm, Abrams and Co. Always dressed chic for the office, she presented well to existing and potential clients and her attention to detail was second to no one. Now twenty-six and lacking the prospect of a husband, she was unaware how active her father was becoming in finding her a mate. Surely, such a charismatic woman should be married and Charles Groder would certainly agree.

One afternoon, Sean, Jennifer, and Charles Groder, a partner in the firm, ate lunch at their regular table at a diner close to the office. Striking up a conversation, Sean asked Jennifer, "How does one go about finding a husband?"

She smiled slyly. "What's this about, Dad?"

"Answer the question."

"Okay. I'll play your game." She rolled her eyes. "First, you make a list."

"Who's on the list?" asked Sean.

Jennifer glanced around the restaurant. "How about him?" She pointed her finger.

Sean and Charles looked up to see a well-dressed, suave gentleman walk by the table at that exact moment. He measured six feet three. His blond hair was slicked back behind his ears. He was a regular at the restaurant, always eating at the next table. Noticing Jennifer's intense gaze, he said, "Hello, did you need something?" He rested his fingers lightly on the table.

Charles waved him off with a gesture of familiarity. "Go eat, Blair."

"Doesn't he work at the bank?" Sean asked.

Charles took a forkful of mashed potatoes. "Yeah."

"What's his name?"

"Blair Whitman," Charles said.

Jennifer played along. "There are other candidates," she said, twirling her fingers on her palm. "Robbie. James. Bill. Mark and Chris."

Sean reached for his day planner to write down the names. "Quite a few names. Any particular order?"

Charles tried to hide his amusement.

Jennifer grinned in the direction of Blair. His face was hidden behind a menu at the next booth. "How about by height? Tallest to shortest."

Sean made more notes in his planner. "Any age requirement?" he asked.

"Over forty is too old," replied Jennifer.

Charles looked over at Blair. "He's got to be about thirty-eight."

"What if two of them are the same height?" Sean asked.

"Then the younger one comes first," Jennifer nodded and went back to her spaghetti, the blue plate special. Sean observed how her attention could switch on and off at a moment's notice. The conversation soon turned to politics.

Sean knew her well. Outwardly, Jennifer had a charm about her. She spoke to others with respect and even admiration when she recognized desirable qualities in those she knew well. However, inside she hid her uncertainty and insecurities. People around her didn't realize the depth of her person, the unique qualities that formed a combination of talent, expertise, empathy and sincerity. She was honest and good in a wonderful way. Only certain people outside her parents knew about her struggles—and her secret. He decided to take the list seriously to find her a match.

Back at work, Sean chuckled to himself about the conversation over lunch. The fact that Blair had passed by their table at that exact moment was an amusing coincidence. Jennifer didn't seem to know Blair that well, but first impressions were important. Of the other names, only one was familiar: Robbie. The others he'd have to look into. Were they fictional or real? He'd soon find out. Sean and Charles spoke about many topics at lunch, including the stock market, current events, the economy, government and international relations. Jennifer was a welcome addition to their table. Her questions and comments were insightful.

He changed his focus and prepared for an important meeting.

About a week later, Sean answered his intercom at the office.

Charles's deep voice came over the speaker. "Sean, I've got something to tell you. Jennifer sent Blair a Valentine's Day card in February."

"How about that? What did it say?"

"Bunch of hearts. Will you be mine? That sort of thing."

"So she's smitten? She's always been forthright but I'm rather surprised she would send such a thing to someone she's hardly spoken to. How did this come about?"

"He said they've crossed paths, but he's never been formally introduced. She must have dropped it off at the bank."

"How did you find out?"

"I've been acquainted with Blair since December last year. He works in investment banking at the bank. I mentioned Jennifer's name to him yesterday and he told me he received a card signed by her."

"Is he genuine? Is he someone suitable for her?" asked Sean.

"Only way to find out is to talk to him. Quiz him a little."

"Jennifer never mentioned she knew anything about him. Maybe we need to set up a meeting."

"How do you do that?" said Charles. He paused. "Isn't Jennifer an artist?"

"An amateur Sunday painter. Why?"

"Her paintings mean a lot to her, right?"

"She's sensitive about her art."

"What if he asked to see some of her work for his new condo? He's moving soon," said Charles. "I'll suggest he inquire about her art."

"Good. Keep me updated." Sean ended the call.

Another day passed. Sean lined up to speak to a teller. Blair spotted him and came out to greet him. "Aren't you Sean Abrams?" Blair asked.

"Hello, how do you know me?" Sean said.

"Everyone knows Abrams and Co. around here. My name's Blair Whitman. I work here as an investment manager. Pleased to meet you." He extended his hand and shook Sean's. "So you are Jennifer's father? A mutual friend told me your daughter paints. Is that correct?"

"Yes, as a matter of fact. Why do you ask?"

"My friend suggested I ask to view her portfolio. I'm moving to a new condominium and need to decorate."

"Blair, I think you need to meet her." Sean moved closer. "Go on a fact-finding mission."

Blair's eyes widened. "What's this about?"

"You need to find out about Jennifer. She's elusive but she's all right. I want to get your impression of her."

"Why? Don't you know your own daughter?"

"Daughters don't always share with their fathers. Talk to her. As a favour to me. It could become very advantageous to do so."

Blair raised a brow. "What's this cloak and dagger bit?"

"She's aloof," Sean said.

"I can see that. I pass her in the street but she never greets me."

"Charles thinks you two would be good together."

"Charles Groder?" Blair looked surprised. "He's the one that told me she's an artist."

Sean smiled to himself at their little ruse.

Blair pulled out a business card and handed it to Sean. "Here's my card. Ask her to text me." Blair walked away, with a slight grin on his face.

"Jennifer." Sean caught her coming in from a coffee break. "I ran into Blair."

Jennifer took off her herringbone coat and hung it in the staff closet. "Blair from the bank?"

"He mentioned he'd like to see your portfolio. He wants to purchase something for his new place."

"You're kidding." She rolled her eyes. "How about a Lawren Harris or a Tom Thomson? That would be a real investment. Has he tried approaching an actual gallery?"

"Just call him."

"There's really no point."

Sean extended his hand, holding Blair's business card. "No hurry. Whenever you like." Jennifer hesitated, and then took the card.

Blair sat at a booth in the diner. He was happy to meet Jennifer formally. It was actually quite funny how this lunch meeting came about. He had run into Sean twice in the last few days, Jennifer called him and now here he was. Sean had spoken to him on the phone and seemed to have a strong interest in his daughter's choice of partner—her future-to-be he called it.

Sean had asked Blair about his background and present situation. Blair had a commerce degree in finance. He'd worked as a teller then moved to investment banking. He'd never been married, had no kids and lived alone. He had one sister married, with an eight-year-old daughter.

Sean suggested to him to keep his distance while interviewing her. He warned him not to make any grand overtures. He must assess Jennifer without any romantic notion. Sean explained it was to develop an understanding of who she was, what she was like.

At the table next to Blair, Charles casually drank a cup of coffee and started on his sole filet.

Blair said, "Charles, can you hear me from there?"

Charles put down his fork, turned his head and said, "How can I not hear you?"

In the next moment, Jennifer appeared in a black tailored suit with a red silk shirt and black pumps, carrying a tablet. She slid into the booth with Blair. "Hello, you're here already."

"Yes, I like punctuality."

"Is this a business lunch, because I didn't bring my credit

card. I only have an hour." Jennifer glanced at her smartphone to check the time.

"Why don't we order before we talk business?"

"Yes, of course." She put down her smartphone and opened a menu. Blair noticed her long manicured fingernails with crimson polish.

The waitress came over. "Would you like coffee?"

"Yes," they said in unison. The waitress poured coffee for both of them and took their order. Blair ordered a steak sandwich with fries. Jennifer ordered the chicken Caesar salad.

Blair watched as Jennifer added two creamers to her coffee. "I should have asked for milk. Less fat." She stirred her coffee and licked the spoon.

"Why two creamers then if you're worried about the fat content?" he asked.

"It sweetens the coffee."

"Why don't you use sugar?"

"Because I like cream."

"But you said—"

"So you want to see my portfolio now?" she interrupted.

"That's why I'm here. I'm moving into a new place and need to decorate."

"That's great." Jennifer held her tablet so Blair could see.

He looked at the first image. "Oh, I like this one."

"That's one of my masterpieces. I don't want to sell that one."

He swiped to the next image on the screen. "How about this one?"

"I gave that one away. I don't have it anymore." She bit her lip.

He flipped through the pages slowly. "These are all so good. You must be academically trained to create these masterpieces."

"They aren't all masterpieces. They're just paintings." She frowned and reached for her water glass.

"How long does it take to paint one of these?"

"It really takes longer than you think. I don't charge by the hour. I charge if it's good enough." She took a large gulp of water.

"What do you charge if it's not good enough?"

"Look, I work full-time. I only paint as a hobby." She visibly began to wilt.

"So you're an amateur."

She pouted. "Yes, I'm an amateur but someday these may be worth something when I'm dead."

"So when you're dead, these will be worth something you think?"

She sighed. "Okay, don't bother. I realize you wanted a look, but there's no obligation to buy."

He thought about the double meaning of her words. "What kind of materials do you use?" He turned another page.

"Acrylic paint. I usually paint on store-bought canvases."

"You don't make your own? You use store-bought canvases."

Her shoulders sagged. "Yes. Any other things you want to know before I pass out?" She looked faint.

He flipped another page. "What's your technique?" he asked. "How do you go about doing this?"

"What do you mean? Like think or contemplate or visualize? What do you mean?" She seemed a little confused.

"You don't know what I mean?" Blair subtly put pressure on her.

"What do you really want to know?" she said, exasperated.

"I'm interested to know if our notions about art are similar," he said. "If we like the same things."

Jennifer's face turned salmon pink. "How's work?"

Blair was silent. He never discussed work. She looked disappointed.

He flipped to the last several pages. "This work is so good. There's a lot here."

"You really think so?" She brightened up a little. "If you'd like, you can come to my house and see the originals. The photographs don't do them justice. You need to see the originals."

Sean observed when Jennifer returned to the office, she was subdued. "How was lunch?"

"Blair made me feel so anxious with his deadpan approach. I don't think he was really interested in my art. Even though he asked questions about the work, I think he was more interested in finding out about me."

"Does he have potential?"

"I don't know, Dad. He was so rigid."

Sean read a little more into what she said. She saw Blair as having potential but she didn't mention the previous conversation regarding finding her a mate. Jennifer had a partial case of amnesia, which affected her short-term and long-term memory. She'd block events out of her mind that weren't useful for her to remember. Her doctor called it a 'selective' memory. She probably hadn't taken that conversation seriously and promptly dismissed it. She also may have forgotten about sending the Valentine's Day card to Blair even though one would think she would remember.

"Don't worry about it. By the way, you look nice today," Sean said.

"Thank you. I spent an hour figuring out what to wear to that meeting. I really would like to sell him a painting."

The next day, Jennifer called in sick. Blair approached Sean and Charles at the diner at lunch hour. Blair said, "Jennifer wants me to come to her place."

"That would be my house," corrected Sean.

"Be a gentleman," Charles said.

"Take it nice and slow, I know. She's a charming girl, but not too experienced I gather. She's sensitive and modest, almost timid," said Blair. "What's your angle, Charles? Why are you in on this?"

Charles looked to Sean. Blair followed his gaze.

"Blair, welcome to the inner circle," Sean said.

Blair sat down next to Charles. "What's the inner circle?"

Jennifer was in a huff. Blair hadn't called in two weeks but she was very hopeful, he'd come by and see her art. After all, he had asked for some prices at their lunch together. He had said that he would like to see the originals, if it wasn't too much trouble. Finally, she decided to call him at work.

"Hello, Blair Whitman, investment banking."

"Hi, I know you're probably busy but I thought you might come over and—"

"Sorry, whom am I speaking to?"

"Ah, forgive me. It's Jennifer Abrams."

"Slow down. Take a breath."

Her heartbeat was rapid. "I was just wondering if you'd like to visit and see my art."

"Let me check my calendar. How about Tuesday evening on the fifth?" he asked.

"That will be fine," she said.

"See you then, Jennifer."

"Bye." After she hung up, she twirled on her toes in excitement.

In anticipation of Blair's visit, she cleaned up her studio and put her paints and brushes away. She swept the floor and arranged her art around the room.

The evening of his anticipated visit, she paced back and forth, constantly looking at the clock. It was almost eight when finally the doorbell rang. She swung the door wide open. "Hello."

"Sorry, I got detained." He took off his shoes in a polite manner and placed his leather gloves on the table in the front hall. She offered to take his coat and hung it in the closet. She led him downstairs to her studio.

"Here we are. This is my studio." She turned on the light. All four walls were covered with paintings in bright, bold colours. They all showed her unique style. She asked, "What's the décor like in your new place?"

"Well, I haven't really seen it. It's still under construction but there's black and grey tile work with cream walls."

"Any of my paintings would brighten up the place."

He frowned. "I forget which ones I was looking at."

She pointed at three paintings. "These are the ones you were interested in."

"I see."

"These are impressionist pieces inspired by Claude Monet. I like to juxtapose various colours to create a sense of light and movement." She spoke about her other interests. She said she was a pop music fanatic and a movie junkie. They went into the next room, where she showed him her CD and DVD collection. A large television and stereo equipment dominated one wall.

"I've seen a lot of those movies." Sean leaned over to read some of the titles of her movie collection.

"Funny, so have I!" She laughed.

Samantha, the family cat, walked into the room and brushed

her tail against Blair's leg.

As Blair kneeled down to pet the cat, he said, "I don't own any original art. I was only interested because it's you."

Outwardly, Jennifer didn't react but inside she did cartwheels. He left shortly after, suggesting that she come over and see his new place after completion. She responded, "Sounds like a good idea."

Chapter 2

Sean knew his daughter could be coy and wanted to educate Blair on Jennifer's needs and idiosyncrasies. She needed a lot of attention. She'd never lived on her own because she was used to being coddled – even at twenty-six. It took her a while to warm up to others. She hadn't dated in years. Sean spoke to Blair at the diner while Jennifer was at a lunch meeting.

Blair commented, "You must be very close to her."

"I know her behaviour, but not necessarily how to help her find answers," Sean replied.

"Answers to what questions?"

"She has her reasons for what she does. I am a little stunned at the course her life has taken. She isn't as she appears."

"I see her as well-protected. She's unsure of herself?"

"Exactly why I think she needs a mate. To support her emotionally and maintain a favourable, stable home situation."

"Not everyone needs a spouse."

"Believe me, she does. She mentioned a total of six possible suitors."

"She's got a list?" Blair furrowed his brow.

Sean let it sink it.

"Where am I on the list?" Blair asked tensely.

"You're her first choice."

"Based on what criteria?"

"Tallest to shortest."

Blair looked at him with disbelief. "Are you serious?"

Sean didn't answer.

"The other nominees," Blair said. "How did they get on the list?"

"They come from varied backgrounds. Two are on disability pensions."

"Why choose a mate who can't work?"

"Because they're mentally ill."

"Why would she choose a mentally ill partner?" Blair frowned.

"Because she's mentally ill."

"Really? I wouldn't have known. Has she been ill for some time? How sick is she?"

Sean shrugged. "She manages well with medication."

"It's not exactly a desirable trait in a spouse."

"She compensates in other ways. I think it's time you met the others."

"To check out the competition?"

"Yes," said Sean.

Punctual as usual, Blair arrived at a meeting room at a local community center. Sean had arranged for the candidates to meet with each other there. He said that it was a neutral environment. Blair didn't know what to expect. Sean said he was confident that he had found the exact people on Jennifer's list, based on his sleuth work and consultations with her circle of friends and associates. When Blair arrived three men were already there. They introduced themselves. Mark wore glasses and a Canucks jersey. Robbie's hair was dark and cropped, and his fingernails were yellow with nicotine. Slouched over a table at the back of the room, Bill had a bony build and a five o'clock shadow. He wore oversized sneakers and fidgeted with a set of keys.

"Where are the other two?" Blair asked.

Robbie replied, "Chris is out in the hall."

"The guy with red hair?" Blair remembered seeing a stocky carrot top outside the room.

"Yeah, that's Chris," Robbie said. Blair noticed his skin was deeply tanned against his cream shirt and light grey shorts. He looked as if like he just flew in from the tropics.

"Why doesn't Chris come in?" said Blair.

"Because he's afraid of getting beat up. He's got paranoid schizophrenia," Robbie said.

Blair asked, "How do you know?"

"Because he told me. James isn't here. He isn't coming."

"Why's that?" said Blair.

"Because his doctor advised him not to come. He's bipolar," answered Robbie.

"How do you come by your information?"

"Let's just say I do my research."

"Well, let's start then. We need to set down some ground rules." Blair cleared his throat. "It's supposed to go by order of height, so I need some leeway time, a head start before any of you decide to muscle in. I'm asking for six weeks. If I don't get results, the next one down the line can ask her out."

The others didn't protest. "Okay, let's double-check for respective heights," Blair said.

"Fine by me," said Mark. The others stood up. "I'm six feet tall."

Blair asked, "You're the next one after me?"

Mark nodded. Robbie stepped to stand next to Mark.

"Then comes you." Blair pointed at Robbie.

Robbie said, "James and I are tied at five eleven, but he's younger so he comes before me if he decides to play."

"And Bill?" Blair pointed at. He shrugged and looked uncomfortable.

"Bill's next," said Mark. "Chris is last."

"Hear that, Chris?" Robbie yelled through the doorway. Chris popped his head in the open doorway then disappeared again.

Robbie said, "Let's talk about who's the most suitable. Who does she love the most?"

Blair said, "I got Valentine's Day card from her. Anybody else have any evidence?"

"Bill knows her the best because he's lived next door to her since they were toddlers. Childhood sweethearts," said Robbie.

"Why are you here, Robbie?" Blair said.

"Because I'm the one that's going to introduce her to Hollywood," Robbie replied.

"Wait a second. Hollywood?" said Blair.

Robbie leaned against a table with his arms crossed. "I don't mind telling you, I have friends and family there. Michael Heedes is my father. I'm sure you recognize his name. He won an Oscar four years ago. I can give her a life within the Hollywood elite with all that entails."

"Can you prove she feels something toward you?" Blair asked.

"She means everything to me. I exchanged letters with her."

"Do you have them with you?"

"No, I don't."

"What's Bill's story?" Blair said.

Bill piped up. "I'm only here because I want to hear what people have to say. I'm not interested in a relationship with her. I'm engaged to someone else."

"What about you, Mark? What's your angle?"

"I'm a friend of a friend. That's how I got to meet her. I'd do anything to help her, but I don't believe she has any feelings for me."

Blair said, "You're on the list. That means something."

"I don't know if it would work out," said Mark.

"Fair enough. Does anyone know James?" Blair said. "Is he in or out?"

Robbie answered. "I'll check it out. I know how to get his number."

"Okay, so it's settled then. Six week intervals," Blair said with finality.

Blair met with Sean privately. "It was mind-boggling. I don't know what she sees in any of them. One was a no-show and another was afraid to enter the room."

"Jennifer has great empathy for all people," said Sean. "I wanted to see yourselves as equals."

"So she could end up with any one of the six?" Blair continued, "The only competition seems to be Robbie. If he exchanged letters with her, why isn't he seeing her already?"

Sean replied, "There's a story behind Robbie. He's witty and popular with the female persuasion. He never had trouble getting a date except for Jennifer. He gets cold feet."

"What's he afraid of?" asked Blair.

"Rejection, infidelity."

"Now that you mention it, I was also thinking along those terms myself. She seems to be attracted to many types. What's to stop her from seeing other men without my knowledge?"

"Trust her." Sean looked him in the eye.

"She's got a list! How can I trust her?" Blair was more than annoyed.

Sean started to call Blair every few days with information and details about Jennifer's personality and personal life. Her favourite colour was violet. Her favourite food was sautéed prawns dipped in melted butter. She liked to swim and tan on the beach. She enjoyed visiting art galleries and going out to the movies. When she talked about art, her eyes would light up.

Sean said, "Feel free to discuss any concerns you may have. Nothing is taboo with me. You are my eyes and my ears."

"Why don't you just talk to her?" said Blair.

"Because I'm her father."

Blair came across Abrams and Co.'s accounts at the bank while covering for someone in the business accounting department. He saw the amounts of cheques made out to Sean. He also came across Sean's investment portfolio quite by accident. A co-worker had left his screen on with the amounts showing. Unintentionally, he discovered that Sean was a millionaire several times over. He had done well with his business and investments. This raised a question in his mind. If Sean were to die, Jennifer could be entitled to inherit millions. He did not discuss his findings with Sean or Charles. This was sensitive material.

Blair was proud to be included in Sean's inner circle. Sean revealed facts he never told anyone. He told stories of cases he won, stories about perjury and judges that put politics above fairness.

On one occasion, Sean had represented an investment manager accused of fraud and embezzlement. He knew he was guilty from the start but fought hard to create doubt in the minds of the jurors. He battled with the ethics of aiding a guilty party to go free without punishment. In the end, he obtained a settlement. The defendant agreed to pay a $100,000 fine and spend no jail time. Sean remarked, "His true punishment came later when he couldn't get a job anywhere and ended up on disability. His back was injured in a car accident."

Blair wondered how often winning a case overruled ethics in Sean's work.

Sean missed lunch at the diner. When Blair asked about his morning. He said, "I was in court. A witness blatantly lied on the stand, contradicting his own sworn statement. He was dismissed. I demanded a mistrial and got it. This will give me more time to formulate my arguments for next time." He never mentioned names, but was glad to speak generally with Blair.

He talked about his reservations about a judge who acted irresponsibly. This judge kowtowed to the political agenda of the majority government. Any cases that had possible negative ramifications on the party in power were assigned to him. On more than one occasion, he vetoed a jury's decision for his own personal gain. Now he was a Supreme Court judge.

Sean thought highly of Blair. He was educated, honest and open. Sean rarely spoke to anyone outside the firm about his experiences as a lawyer. He felt by sharing information with Blair, they could develop a mutual trust.

Sean weighed the other candidates against Blair. Sean decided Blair had to be the one. The others would not be able to hold her interest, keep her safe, and support her in her current lifestyle. Robbie had money but Sean didn't think he'd come through.

Sean met Blair one day at the diner while Jennifer was downtown hand-delivering an important document. The waitress brought them coffee.

"When do I make my move?" Blair asked.

"Hold off for now. You need to prepare. You have to spend a lot of time with her. Leave her up to her own agenda during the day, but be good to her. She doesn't cook. You know that?"

"How will we eat if she doesn't cook?"

"You'll have to figure that out." Sean sipped his coffee.

"She could learn by necessity. I can't see her scrubbing the floors with nails like those."

"Have you thought about children?" Sean asked Blair.

"No, I haven't. Actually, aren't we putting the cart before the horse? She and I aren't even dating yet."

"She never discusses it. I think she fears she would pass on certain genes and her children would develop schizophrenia. It's wishful thinking on my part she would decide to have at least one."

"She's your only child. I could see why you'd want grandchildren. What if Jennifer decides against me? What if we don't click?" Blair said.

"I'm betting on you. You're the only one of the six, I would trust with my life. If she doesn't come willingly, we'll use coercion as a last resort."

"But that's not right."

"It's going to work out. I know my daughter. You're the one, understand?"

"I understand."

Blair went home that day with feelings of conflict. He wondered if he was more in love with the Abrams' estate rather than focusing on Jennifer. He saw her twice and already he was thinking about wedding rings and colour schemes that would suit Jennifer as well as himself. He wanted to call her, but Sean warned him to limit contact for the time being.

Blair got a surprise visit from James one morning at work. He just waltzed into his office.

"Hi, I'm James." He wore an old army jacket and faded jeans. His dark brush cut had no hint of a curl. He wore a large gold ring with his initials engraved on it: J.J. Blair thought he looked like a younger version of Robbie.

"Sorry, but I don't know you," Blair said.

"Yes, you do. I'm on the list." He reached into his pocket for his cellphone.

"Well, hello. Can I get you a cup of coffee?" Blair asked. He was a little astounded.

"No, thanks." James sat down and punched his cellphone. "Hello, Robbie? I'm in. Okay, sure." He hung up.

"You just phoned Robbie?"

James sat back in the chair facing Blair's desk. "He told me to come here."

"Well, pleased to meet you." Blair shook his hand. "How can I be of service?"

"I think it's the other way around. I talked to my psychiatrist and I decided it's against my better interest to get involved with Jennifer. I just started a new job. I can barely afford things as it is. She's in a different class altogether."

Blair sat back and said, "How do you know her?"

"From the mental health team."

"Oh, so you see her there on a regular basis?"

"No, not anymore. I'm working." The ringtone on James' phone started to play. He flipped it open. "Yes, I understand." He clicked the phone. "Robbie's across the street. I'm supposed to meet him after this." James looked agitated. "Stand up and turn around."

"I beg your pardon?" Blair raised an eyebrow.

"I'm here to check you out. Do it and I'll leave."

Blair stood up and turned around.

"Not bad. But you need to own a pair of jeans. Like these." He pointed to his Levi's. "Make sure they hug your ass. You see these shoes?" He pointed at his brown laced-up leather boots. "I paid a hundred and eighty-five dollars for these and I get compliments all the time. You need the right shoes."

"Thanks for the advice, but why are you suggesting changes to my wardrobe?"

"I know Jennifer, and she likes a good-looking guy. You've got to loosen up."

Blair played along with him. "What about the hair?" Blair pointed to his well-groomed head of hair.

"That's cool, a little conservative. Well, I got to go. Robbie said a maximum of five minutes."

Blair sat down after James left the office. He was speechless.

James took the elevator down, lit a cigarette outside the bank and went across the street to where Robbie waited with his own smoke.

Robbie said, "What do you think of him?"

James shrugged. "Out of my league financially. He's got to be twice my age."

"To me he's got it made. I don't think Jennifer has any intention of dating everyone on that list. She's smart."

"Yeah, but she has schizophrenia. Mind you, she keeps it under control through medication. But what if she relapses? Can he can handle that?"

"He's going to find out." Robbie pulled out another cigarette after flicking the last butt.

"How did you find me anyway?" said James.

"I have a lot of connections. A couple of well-placed calls and I can locate almost anybody. You're lucky. You're ahead of me."

"Fuck the order. If you want her badly enough, just go ahead and ask her for a date," said James.

Robbie shook his head. "It isn't that easy. I know for a fact she's inexperienced. It could turn into a fiasco if more than one of us is having sex with her."

"Worried about pregnancy, VD or something?"

"No, I'm worried if she's blitzed, her head will start to spin. She wouldn't know up from down. She'd be confused and withdraw from all of us. She scares easily."

"C'mon. She's an apple ready to be picked. Test the waters."

Robbie kicked a parking meter. "I could have had her years ago but I was dealing with my own problems."

"Drugs?" James flicked ashes off the end of his cigarette.

"How'd you know?" Robbie asked. James shrugged. "I was into crack. Charged on breaking and entering." Robbie paused and looked up at the sky. "I'll never have her."

"Are you off crack now?" James asked.

"Yeah, now I just drink and smoke."

James laughed. "Could be worse."

Sean had researched the six in fair detail, building a profile of each one. Robbie's life was like something out of the movies. When he was five, his parents divorced. His mother Laura filed papers after she walked into the bedroom and caught her husband Michael naked with a teenage actress. His mother gained custody. She and Robbie moved to Vancouver away from their previous home in Los Angeles. She had wanted to raise him in a stable environment outside of the limelight. Robbie asked her why they got married in the first place if their personalities were the opposite of each other. She replied, "Because I was pregnant with you."

Michael saw Robbie about five times a year. When he did something wrong, Michael would hit or slap him. He would say, "'Fess up and I'll be easy on you." He took him on vacations to Tahiti, Fiji and Mexico. He gave him money to spend and plenty of alcohol and cigarettes – even when he was underage. His mother disapproved of Michael's attitude toward Robbie, but he had rights to see him. Michael saw Robbie less after he got older. He spent most of his time with young fashion models, working on films and jet-setting in Hollywood.

When Robbie was sixteen, he got suspended from school for

fighting with another student. He cut him with a Swiss army knife. When asked why he did it, he said the other student called him names. His mother started him on a home schooling program, but he failed his high school equivalency exam for lack of interest. He took jobs waiting tables. He was embittered serving customers, day after day. But by his own efforts, he made it as far as restaurant manager. His father gave him extra money, which he spent on drugs and alcohol until he went into rehab.

Sean believed Robbie's drug and alcohol abuse stemmed from his relationship with his father and broken family life. Perhaps he wanted acceptance from his father and never received it. Or felt robbed that he didn't live in Hollywood among the rich and famous with Michael. Despite his controversial behaviour, Michael was still a star.

Sean knew why he was on the list because of letters she wrote him. When Jennifer first got ill she was in love with Robbie. They knew each other from school but never really spoke face to face. He was her obsession. At the time, he was popular at school. Jennifer, on the other hand, was a very shy, inhibited teenager. Robbie tried to talk to her a couple of times, but she'd shy away without a word. She rarely spoke to classmates or teachers. As her illness worsened, she stopped communicating with her teachers and peers. She became more and more isolated and continued to build an imaginary world around Robbie and herself.

So when Robbie turned sixteen and was suspended, she ceased to see him at school. Instead she developed a fantasy life about him. She sent four letters to his home, professing her love and hinting at marriage. He was nonplussed about it and told all his friends to stay away from her. He wrote her back in large capitalized print, asking her to meet him after school. For some reason, she never showed up. In the end, he never actually walked her home or carried her books. He knew it was a long shot but he hoped she would keep her word and marry him in the future. Mrs. Abrams found letters from Robbie under Jennifer's bed while vacuuming. Sean glanced at them briefly, stressing they needed to know the contents in order to protect her.

Chris's situation was quite different. He was divorced and had his own daughter. He worked in construction and odd jobs to make enough money for him and his daughter to live. He sacrificed to maintain custody of his daughter. He met Jennifer through an art workshop they both attended. They immediately hit it off and texted on occasion. They ran into each other a few times. He was curious how the situation with Jennifer would play out. He knew Mr. Abrams was very influential and asked to meet him one time. After about five minutes, Chris laid his cards on the table. He stated, "I really like Jennifer but she told me flat out, 'No one gets to me but through my father.'"

Sean asked, "What can you do for her?" Chris outlined his various interests and abilities. Then Sean said, "You're out of time." Then Chris stomped out of the office.

From Chris's point of view, the meeting between the suitors was an eye opener but also seemed very out of place. The stakes seemed pretty high for a woman like Jennifer. She was so modest and down to earth. Why all the fuss? She was attractive, but she lived with her parents and hardly went out. Certainly there were easier fish to catch.

Mark had other woman acquaintances but he wasn't attached at the moment. He recently started a new business doing web design and custom-building computers for customers. He had an extensive knowledge of computer software and hardware. Because he was involved in a lot of sports and had many friends, he really didn't have time or energy to think about dating Jennifer. He knew she had emotional problems due to her mental illness. She was a friend, but not the kind that turned into a lover.

Bill had known Jennifer the longest of six candidates. He had lived next door to her since they were three. He actually kept a photo of them kissing on the front stoop as kids. In the past, he had a thing for her, but recently he had proposed to a wonderful Australian girl. He planned to move there soon. He was curious about how Jennifer's situation would pan out, but he had his own concerns. His Australian girlfriend was pregnant.

James generally took things in stride. He didn't really have a problem making female friends. But when he met Jennifer at the mental health team, he was blown away. She walked in wearing a black suede coat, high-heeled leather boots and jewelry that must have cost a fair bit. Her hair, make-up and nails were immaculate. She smiled and sat down next to him. They introduced themselves and got into a discussion about symptoms they had in common. She was very hot in his book. But she was seven years older than he. She seemed to back off a little when he came close. She'd turn her head or look down at the carpet. There was some unspoken distance even though she seemed to thoroughly enjoy his company. He had her phone number on a business card she gave him, but never used it.

Chapter 3

Blair met Sean after work for a discussion at the diner. Sean treated him to coffee.

"I feel subordinate in this situation. I don't like being a number so to speak. What else makes Jennifer so important about her that she's got a list, for chrissakes?" Blair said. "What the hell is going on?"

Sean paused and folded his fingers together. "Is it important to help other people become successful?" asked Sean.

"I guess. Never really thought about it."

"Do you like pop music?"

"Not particularly. Just certain songs I like," Blair said.

"What do people do if they can sing and play music but can't write lyrics?"

Blair leaned back. "You get a songwriter."

"If you could write lyrics for other people's successes, would you do it?"

Blair did a double take. "Are you saying Jennifer's a lyricist?"

Sean nodded.

Blair's eyes got big. "So Jennifer is a closet lyricist who has schizophrenia to boot? That's completely ridiculous. Don't lie to me."

"Jennifer was a very bright child. Intelligence-wise, she was above average. As she got older, she'd record her voice or jot down lyrics. When she realized she had become mentally ill, she offered herself as a research model in order to find better treatments and possible preventions. She wanted to fund the research as well."

"This is incredulous!" Blair said. "No one in their right mind would do that. Why would someone do that? What would she gain?"

Sean replied, "She realized she had more than enough money and her future was financially secure and wanted to contribute to society."

"You mean because she's your only child, she'd inherit your

wealth?"

Sean said, "Not exactly. Her lyrics paid off but the public doesn't know she wrote them. Royalties, my friend."

"So this actually took place? She's a guinea pig in the name of science?"

"She knew there were steps to finding better treatments. Scientific proof is necessary before acceptance into the medical arena. She's worked with the project for ten years."

"Does Charles Groder know about this?" Blair asked.

"He knows I want her to marry. I've confided in him but he doesn't know all the details about the project."

"Does Jennifer have any idea of what could cure schizophrenia? Is a cure even possible?"

"She predicts the solution is a combination of ingredients that are already in the market but untested for schizophrenia treatments. She suggested growth hormone could possibly be a link to finding a cure based on the hypothesis that malnutrition can contribute to psychosis."

Blair rubbed his brow. "So her songwriting is funding mental health research."

"No, it isn't."

"But you said she's funding it." Blair looked puzzled.

"I said that she wanted to fund it. But her offer was refused because of conflict of interest. The federal and provincial government in conjunction with various other private organizations funds the project. By working jointly with drug companies and their researchers, we hope a cure can be found within the next twenty years."

"That's a tall order. There are so many variables. This must be completely under wraps because I see no evidence in the news. I don't know if I believe you."

"It's secret right now. But it's going to come to head. Our effort is to keep a rein on media coverage until it can be seen in the best light."

"Is it ethical to experiment on a human?"

"I've gone over the ethics of this many times. She volunteered and wasn't coerced. It's for the common good. It's how it's publicized."

"Controversy versus an attainable cure."

"Exactly."

"But in order for this to be exposed, they must have successes. Otherwise it's meaningless."

"The government wants to protect itself and I want to protect my daughter. If this blows up, it could be devastating." Sean sighed. "So you see, Blair, why there's a list?"

"Yes, I see why there's a list."

After leaving work, Blair drove to his apartment. He was in the preliminary stages of packing up his belongings to move to the new condo. Unfortunately, there had been some delays by the carpenters and they were waiting for custom orders to complete the kitchen and bathrooms.

He zapped leftovers in his microwave and turned on the television. He flipped channels with his remote for a while then he started thinking about Robbie's comments about Hollywood. Robbie had said that he could introduce Jennifer to a life in Hollywood. He thought about the numerous DVDs in Jennifer's possession besides the music CDs she owned. What else could she write if she had more than a talent for songwriting? Could she write stories or treatments for Hollywood? Surely, Robbie would be a valuable asset to Jennifer should she decide to move into either arena in the future as a legit writer. Right now, she was definitely an unknown, regardless of how many songs she had ghostwritten. It would be hard for her to break into the mainstream now. He couldn't imagine the confusion that would result from an exposé of her secret life – as a writer or as a research model.

The media would have a field day with her when this was over but would it ever be over for Jennifer if what Sean said were true? He worried how she would react to being under the microscope of the public eye. Sean mentioned how much effort Jennifer put into coping with her mental illness. It was more difficult than one would think, battling a mental illness while dealing with the everyday stresses at work. Sean said he admired the way she had achieved so much already. Blair felt he was in a very unique situation. Sean hinted he would set up an allowance for Jennifer's care to be deposited into Blair's bank account if and when they wedded. Blair remained silent in regards to the offer.

Blair waited for the day he could ask Jennifer out formally.

Because of the parameters of the research, Sean requested Blair not to act right now. He explained, because of legal reasons around guardianship, she could not marry until the study was over. If Blair became romantically involved with her prematurely, there could be complications. Right now, she was safe under the roof of her family home. The research took precedence in her life right now. Because of the nature of the project, the government and her family were morally and legally obligated to care for her until her death. Sean said that was the reason why the Abrams lived in Vancouver. The study was restricted within the boundaries of the health authority.

Blair was trying to decide on a bedroom carpet. He wanted to get Jennifer's opinion on colour choice but she had not spoken to him since he visited her house. He was having doubts about how to approach her. He didn't even know if she was attracted to him based on her behaviour. He decided it was her turn to make a move. Why didn't she call him? His nose was out of joint. Instead he called Sean to share his frustration. "You can't get blood out of a stone."

Sean paused, then said, "Why don't you call the others and see where they're at?"

Blair started to call around to the other five. One by one he was told they had all defaulted for different reasons. James said that he didn't think a relationship with Jennifer would work out because he was so much younger. It didn't seem right to him. Mark said there was no romantic attraction between him and her. Chris said that the competition was too tough. Bill had left for Australia. Robbie's personal issues made it highly unlikely he could approach Jennifer.

Blair breathed easier knowing the others had defaulted. Momentarily, he felt like he had won the lottery. The euphoria passed quickly. It was beyond him why men ran from her, so to speak. He decided it was her tendency to distance herself from others. He had already made concessions in his life, cutting back any romantic involvement with anyone else. He waited patiently for the go-ahead but in reality was nowhere with her. Jennifer had an invisible wall around her. It seemed no one could get close to her.

The next week, Blair got a phone call that left him very annoyed. Dr. Jackson, a health official advised he needed to get a physical examination including testing for venereal diseases and HIV. At first, he refused and was ready to hang up. Dr. Jackson said, "In the interest of the safety of Ms. Abrams, we're asking you to undergo a physical. To protect her, we need to rule out any chance of exposure to sexually transmitted diseases as well as any other diseases. This is in no way to reflect badly on you, Mr. Whitman. It's procedure."

Blair was disgruntled but reluctantly agreed to go for testing.

"You will have to repeat the test in three months time. If all tests are negative, you will be free to proceed."

Blair rubbed his brow when he got off the phone. The whole thing was turning into a headache.

Obediently, Blair went to the clinic for testing. He was running in circles and Jennifer still hadn't called him. At the clinic, he was to answer several questions including sexual activity over the past six months. He confessed he had sex twice in the past six months. The doctor asked if he had unprotected sex. At this point, Blair felt extremely uncomfortable. This was really too much for him. He admitted to using a condom one time and not the other. "Why not the latter?" asked the doctor.

"Because Kelly and I date on and off and we know each other pretty well."

After the completed tests, he went to the office for the remainder of the day. It was so humiliating. He sat there feeling rather guilty. Ten days after he visited Jennifer at her house, he and Kelly, a co-worker, had drinks at his apartment. He was feeling a little heat and seduced Kelly.

The morning after, he had seen Kelly in the coffee room at the bank.

Kelly said, "Fun evening, wasn't it?"

"I'm sorry. I just lost control."

"Hey, it takes two to tango." She smiled then took a sip of coffee. "You look a little rough. Are you okay?"

No answer.

Looking a little hurt, she walked away from the coffeemaker and back to her desk. She eyed him as he passed by her cubicle. He ignored her gaze, crossed the floor and entered his office. He drew the blinds. He admitted to himself he only had sex with Kelly because he was having difficulty with the Jennifer problem.

At work, he spoke abruptly with clients and staff alike. He really didn't like being under a microscope by anyone. The way the government treated him irked the hell out of him. He decided there was no way he was going to contact Jennifer unless she made a move. He found it beneath him to be poked and prodded, submitting to the demands of strangers. He immersed himself in work and put her out of his head.

Chapter 4

Jennifer experienced her own problems. Obsessive and paranoid thoughts bothered her for days at a time. She had bouts of amnesia and loss of concentration. Such was the course of her illness. Sometimes she was right as rain; other times she had breakthrough symptoms and couldn't keep up with her daily routine. She depended on medication in order to cope. She hoped she would be cured someday.

She had a lot of déjà vus. When she listened to popular music over a period of time, the music became so familiar to her she could not separate it from herself. She believed she was a ghostwriter of song lyrics. She couldn't differentiate between the work of other writers and what was possible within her own capabilities. Despite inconsistencies, she had believed her creator fantasy was real. During these phases, she got angry about not being recognized for her work while others claimed the limelight without her. She had no real evidence. No royalties, no credits. Unchecked, the delusions would grow causing her to experience manic and paranoid episodes. Her psychiatrist would increase her medication periodically, which would reduce her obsessive thinking. When she was well, she did not have these beliefs. It was very strange to her.

Jennifer's psychiatrist, Dr. Hutchinson, had met with her ever since her first diagnosis. He consistently denied Jennifer's claim that she was a ghostwriter. He denied she should experience any malcontent over not being recognized, as she had no proof she wrote any lyrics. Instead he led her to believe these ideas were part of her illness. In meetings with other doctors and therapists at the clinic, he discussed the handling of the case. He felt privacy and confidentiality were overruled by necessity. It was possible, circumstances could change and Jennifer would need to see someone else. The history behind her case was complicated and certain specifics were not included in his monthly reports.

One day he was speaking to Dr. Camen and Dr. Handel, two

associates in the research project. "Jennifer's imbalance is one of perception. She believes, on one hand, she is a creative genius of epic proportions to the extreme and on the other hand, she's an inferior mentally ill person who is a liability to society."

Dr. Camen said, "She needs to level out."

"Exactly right," Dr. Hutchinson said. "She holds the key to her own happiness and well-being. If she doesn't change her self-perception she will never be content."

"Is it right to claim her achievements are false? Should she not be allowed to know about her genius if it is true?" asked Dr. Camen.

"No." Dr. Hutchinson shook his head. "She's at a point where her grandiose thoughts get out of control. She needs to deflate her mania and at the same time elevate her self-esteem to a realistic level. Under no circumstances, am I going to let it out of the bag until she gets a grip on herself."

"So the reality is someplace in between."

"Yes. I believe she's capable of getting there."

Dr. Handel said, "I'm fully behind her one hundred percent. We all want a cure."

"Don't hold your breath. She's got a way to go before she hits normalcy. As a team, we need to keep chipping away at her until she can accept moderate achievement levels."

Jennifer spent less time at work and more time in her studio. She arranged to work only a three-day week. She found it too difficult to work at the office full-time because of sedation from her medication. Instead, she focused on a new series of paintings and fiddled on the computer. She wanted to prove she could write. That was her new goal. She was tired of typing reports. She wanted to write something original. Her first drafts of poems and prose were pretty rough. She was pretty rusty after only typing for lawyers for years. But she felt she must still have the ability if she had it before.

She knew her fantasies about ghostwriting a large body of work seemed impossible. No one could write so much at a young age. She couldn't pinpoint when or how she came up with lyrics – but the belief still gnawed at her. She had a tendency to blow things out of proportion. Perhaps she wasn't responsible for such a large number of songs. What if she only wrote half, or a third or a tenth of what she thought?

She discussed with her parents about her desire to become a writer. Her mother said nothing, just nodded her head. Sean said, "If it means something to you, do it."

She buckled down to write on a regular basis.

One day at a store, James was buying spray paint and ran into Jennifer. They decided to have coffee and then walk over to the pier.

"How's the painting going?" asked James.

"Oh, fine. How about yours?"

James stretched. "I gave one to a girlfriend of mine."

"You never mentioned her before."

"It was nothing serious." He played with his stir stick. The coffee was too bitter for his taste.

Jennifer looked out at the seagulls over the water. "It's interesting we have so much in common."

"Like what?" James asked.

"Like we're both mentally ill, single and artists." Jennifer smiled, giving him the eye.

They talked about the weather, about living in Vancouver and about experiences they had. James came from South Carolina. He lived in various places across North America before moving to Vancouver about six years ago. It was home to him. Jennifer shared a little about her loneliness because she didn't have any close friends.

It started to drizzle so they parted. James waved goodbye and walked to the bus stop. He pulled out his cellphone and called Robbie. "Hi, Robbie?"

"What's up?" Robbie answered. "I'm in traffic. Make it quick."

"I just had coffee with Jennifer."

"Congratulations. What of it?"

"She asked me a lot of personal questions. She seemed different, more assertive. She actually looked me in the eye and opened up. I think she has the hots for me. I want to be reinstated on the list. Whom do I contact?" James saw the bus approaching in the distance.

"Call the local mental health authority."

"The one in charge of her case? Dr. Tom Hutchinson?" asked James.

"That's the one."

James boarded the bus.

Chapter 5

Bill walked into the kitchen. From the window, he could see the roofline of the Sydney Opera House. The sky was beautiful and clear. The weather was fabulous down under. Emma, his fiancée, poured tea. They were housed temporarily at her parents' home at least until the wedding. He didn't have a work visa, so legally he couldn't work. He had no luck finding work under the table either. Finances were tight for the wedding. He felt the jitters already.

Emma passed him a cup of tea. "Good morning, honey." They kissed. Bill noticed she wore a gold necklace with a heart pendant.

"That's a nice necklace. Is it new?"

Surprised, she covered the pendant with her hand. "I got it several months ago."

"I've never seen you wear it. Did someone give it to you?"

She looked out the window and didn't answer.

"Emma, did you hear me?" Bill repeated his question.

She looked down at the linoleum. "It's from Taylor who introduced us."

"Oh, Taylor in Vancouver. I didn't know you two were that close."

Emma still wouldn't look at him. "We were very close."

Bill heard warning bells going off. "Emma." He pulled her to face him. "Did you have a relationship with him?"

Emma tried to pull away. "It was only one time." Tears came to her eyes.

Bill held on so tight he crushed her arms. "When?"

Emma bawled. "He didn't want to marry me."

Bill said, "Is he the father?"

"I don't know."

"Tell me the truth. Is he or isn't he?"

She nodded ever so slightly.

"Why did you lie, Emma?"

Emma wiped away the tears. "You said you wanted to have a family someday. That's what you said."

"Yeah, my own family, not the leftovers from another relationship. This affects everything."

"No one has to know. I only told you because I thought you honestly loved me regardless of being the biological father or not. You can still be a dad."

"This is sheer manipulation. I came halfway across the globe to be with you."

"I know that." Her voice shook.

'I need to think this over. I'm so furious right now."

She wrapped her arm around his waist. "If it helps any, I want you to know I love you."

Bill pushed her away, strode out of the kitchen and into the den, slamming the door. Emma wailed and tried the door but he locked it. "Please Bill, let me in!" She banged on the door, but Bill ignored her.

Instead he decided to check his email on the computer. His inbox had two new messages: one from his mother, another from Robbie. He read the email from his mother, saying she was going to send them an early wedding present. He didn't reply.

He clicked the mouse and Robbie's message came up. It said, "James is reinstated. He's going for it. The rumour is Jennifer is getting part of her inheritance soon in the neighbourhood of 100,000 dollars."

Bill gulped. Jennifer was going to be a rich lady. He thought about all the borrowing he and Emma needed for their wedding. Jennifer could put him on easy street. He thought about the dead-end jobs he had before, his constant struggle with rent payments and lack of funds when he didn't even have a phone. It was tough going if he stayed in Australia until he could get a work visa or permanent residency. He knew he couldn't support Emma and pay off their debts until he got a good steady job. Emma wanted to stay home with the baby and not work outside the home. He had just enough money now to fly back to Vancouver. He called Robbie long distance.

"It's not everyday I get a call from Australia." Robbie was in good humour. He was fascinated by the chase. He relished the interest around Jennifer. He thought the competition was a hoot.

"Why is James reinstated?" asked Bill.

"Because they had coffee."

"And that's a reason?"

Robbie laughed.

"Why does she have a list anyway? There must be some reason why there are six. Why not three or four?"

"She's playing the field."

"You seem to have a lot of information. Don't you have anything better to do then spread gossip and pester people?" asked Bill.

"I have a lot of time. I make it my business to know what's going on," Robbie said.

"Tell me about the money she's inheriting."

"It isn't an inheritance. It's her money," Robbie said.

"Why the lie?"

Robbie put out his cigarette in an ashtray on his desk and changed the phone to the other ear. "It's a big cover-up. She's a sensation. That's all I can say."

"Are you saying she either won the lottery or she has a secret financier?" asked Bill.

"It's funny you said that. Blair's a financier."

"The money is Blair's?"

"No, that was a lame joke. She got the money through other means."

"Spill it," said Bill.

"She earned it," said Robbie.

"How can you be so sure?"

"She wrote me a letter about it in high school. She's not really crazy. I think she has a split personality."

Robbie used information to trade for other information. He had a way to get people to open up. He harassed Blair on occasion by phone just to cause trouble. He kept tabs on James especially because if James got to Jennifer, he was next. Besides, James was similar in appearance and manner: same height, look, dark hair, and cigarette habit. He felt James was a younger version of himself. Robbie's obsessive behaviour was so strong that he needed to be on anti-anxiety medication. He rarely drank alcohol in combination with the prescription drugs he took. But when he did, he became sedated to the point of falling off barstools or needing a cab home. In a way, he saw Jennifer as his possible salvation. She could set him on the right track. He needed a miracle to save himself.

"Emma, I need to speak to you," Bill said softly from outside the closed bedroom door. He tried the door but it was locked. He knocked. Bedsprings squeaked then footsteps. Emma unlocked the door and let him in. "I have a confession to make," Bill said.

She folded her arms, but didn't speak.

"I'm reinstated on the list for Jennifer," he said.

Emma recoiled. "You told me you weren't even interested in her! You told me it was all a stupid idea to have a waiting list for a marriage partner. She doesn't care about you. I met her when we were by your parents' place in Vancouver. She has nothing in common with you. Why do you want to be on the stupid list again?"

"There must be some reason for me to be on the list."

She rolled her eyes.

"You have your nose out of joint after lying to me about who the father was. How dare you criticize my actions?" Bill said.

"I want the baby to have a father."

"Let's compromise. We'll call off the wedding and live together until the baby is born. If or when my turn comes up, I have the right to fly back and pursue a relationship with Jennifer."

"This is nonsense. Do you love her or me?"

Bill was confused. He did love Emma on some level and had happily anticipated a future with her, but now he had this gnawing emotion that to be with Jennifer would be better. It could be a dream come true. He envisioned a life of opulence with Jennifer ironing his shirts, married and living in a mansion. "I love you both," he said.

Emma threw a pillow at him. "I'm pregnant! You asked me to marry you!" She choked back tears.

He put his arms around her, but she backed away. "I'm here, I'm here," he said. She stopped resisting. He curled on the bed with her in his arms. He wanted to make her feel better. "I'm just doing it for the money. That's all I want from her." Emma sobbed louder.

Sean knew of Robbie's behavioural patterns. He had his own

share of phone calls and email messages from him. If he was available, he always took the calls just to know firsthand what Robbie was up to. Sean knew Robbie to be a live wire, unstable at times. When Jennifer was diagnosed with schizophrenia at the age of sixteen, she talked about Robbie a lot back then, building a delusional fascination around him. Sean wanted to know the truth of their relationship in order to separate her delusion from reality. He spoke to her school counselor who asked Robbie's mother if Sean could meet Robbie. They met in the counselor's office unbeknownst to Jennifer. At the time, Robbie barely knew her. Sean asked him some questions and talked about Jennifer.

Robbie shared openly with Sean because he was attracted to Jennifer. He said after his fight with another student and his suspension from school, he received a note from Jennifer, the first of four. It read, "Are you away for long? I dream about you all the time. Miss you. Love, Jennifer." Robbie said his bipolar diagnosis wasn't right. He believed he wasn't ill at all.

Back then, Sean worried about contact between Robbie and Jennifer. They were both imbalanced and he thought they might get into trouble. Sean and the school counselor decided Robbie was to stay away from the school and Jennifer's house. He was not to speak to or contact her in anyway.

Dr. Hutchinson had told Sean that Robbie and Jennifer's mutual attraction was similar to mammals that mate in the wild. Biologically, they call out for each other. They have a sixth sense about each other. It was uncanny.

Dr. Hutchinson said to Sean, "I believe if they have a relationship, it would either snowball out of control, triggering bizarre manic behaviour in both or else there is an outside chance that they would react favourably and compensate each other's needs. At this point, they fear each other despite mutual attraction."

Sean asked him, "What's the chance Jennifer might suddenly recover by bonding with him? After all, her obsessions began with Robbie in school."

Dr. Hutchinson replied, "I recommend keeping them apart until her mental health and emotions are under control. Otherwise, they may just set each other off, become volatile and someone might get hurt."

"Is it realistic to expect them not to communicate other than through letters? When they are adults, won't they be free to make their own decisions?"

"Jennifer is under the jurisdiction of the government. If we must, we will give Robbie a standing order to remain at a distance from her at all times. He will be contained. Remember, right now they're still developing."

Chapter 6

One morning, Sean was opening his mail. Among the letters from clients, there was one envelope addressed simply, "To Sean Abrams." He opened it and read the contents in bold letters:

I'm tired of hearing what you want. Here's what I want. A wife who works, not a homebody, earns an annual salary no less than $20,000, no more than $30,000. No candy ass excuses she can't cook. No pretentious, stupid art. Knows her place. Mrs. Abrams says Jen never liked bankers. Blair.

Annoyed, Sean chucked the letter aside. He'd deal with it later. He had to take care of another matter.

The next day, Blair called Sean when he received a photocopy of the letter delivered to him by courier. He said, "Sean, believe me. I didn't write this."

"I didn't think you did," said Sean.

"Who wrote it?"

"I'm sure it's Robbie's handwriting." He recognized the capital lettering matched Robbie's letters to Jennifer that Mrs. Abrams found under her bed.

"Insidious. Isn't that harassment?"

Sean didn't answer.

"I haven't seen Jennifer for awhile. How is she?" asked Blair.

"Fine."

"Any progress in her illness?"

"I'll keep you posted. By the way, my wife says you're the one despite what the letter said."

"Thanks for the vote of confidence."

"We'll keep this letter under wraps. I don't want this getting out."

"That's for certain. Thanks for letting me know." Blair hung up.

Later, Blair arrived back in the office after a meeting when Shandele, a co-worker confronted him. "Who is Jennifer Abrams? She left her number for you to return her call. Sounded like it wasn't a business call."

Blair hung up his coat. "She's a friend of mine. Casual acquaintance."

"Does Kelly know who she is?" Shandele folded her arms and leaned against the desk.

"What is that supposed to mean?"

Shandele tapped the desk with her index finger. "We all think you are great husband material. I just want to find out who she is for Kelly's sake."

"This is personal."

"Is Kelly going to be hurt again? She tells me things. I'm sure Jennifer is a nice person. Don't get me wrong. I'm just worried about Kelly's feelings."

"It's none of your business. Kelly is fine. And besides, how would you know anything about Jennifer? You never met her."

"I can pick up a lot from a twenty-second conversation. It was her tone. She comes across genuinely. She also mentioned arranging a time to see your new condo. I just think you better watch whom you're stepping on."

"I'm not discussing this with you. Leave my office." Blair glared at her. She spun on a heel and walked out. The conversation had rattled him. It wasn't Shandele's business. He decided to bring it up with a male co-worker, someone he could trust.

"Say, Eugene. May I discuss something with you in private?"

Eugene looked up from his desk. "Close the door behind you."

"Thanks." Blair entered, closed the door and sat down across from Eugene. "I've got a staff problem. There appears to be some resentment from Shandele about my personal affairs. I'm just starting to know this person that I like, and Shandele confronted me. She says she's looking out for Kelly's interest because I used to see her socially."

Eugene leaned closer. "Don't give me all the details. Just ask me what you need to know."

"I don't want this tiff to interfere with work. I want the freedom to see whom I want, when I want, without it interfering in the office."

"Is it over with Kelly?" Eugene asked.

"It's on again, off again. She's comfortable, no strings attached. She's bailed me out a couple of times."

"Bailed you out how?"

"Difficult situations. Other relationships that didn't work out." Blair adjusted his collar.

"So you turn to her for comfort."

"Yes, and she forgives me every time. She's considerate. Never makes demands on me. I'm sorry this sounds awful on my part."

"You need to sort out your life. If you want to continue to work here, you have to sort out what Kelly means to you. Is this new person a potential client?"

"Jennifer is going to come into some money. She could become a very good client, but that isn't my primary interest."

"Sort out your life. We have policies around relationships between staff. You should abide by them."

"We are also consenting adults, not children in the sandbox."

"What you do is your affair, but if it affects the work, it's wrong." Eugene closed the ledger in front of him and folded his fingers. Blair said thanks and left.

That evening, Blair didn't go out. He didn't call Jennifer back. He wanted to sort out this issue with Kelly before he called Jennifer. He counted the number of times he and Kelly had slept together. He was guilty of stringing her along on several occasions. He visualized how the conversation would go if he were to end it with Kelly. No doubt she'd complain, protest, and put him through the ringer. He went to bed after one after composing what he needed to say.

The next morning, he met her at the coffeemaker in the break room.

"Did you speak to Shandele yesterday?" he asked.

"I hear you have a new girl." Kelly was curt, but that was her natural manner. She reached for a carrot muffin from a tray on the counter, changed her mind and took a brownie.

"May I speak to you in my office?"

"This should be interesting." They walked into his office and he closed the door. "What's this about, Blair?"

"I may have to end our relationship for good." He sat down in his executive chair and picked up a fountain pen. He put it down again.

"You mean you finally found the love of your life?" She smiled, fluttered her eyelashes and leaned over the desk.

"I know we haven't always seen eye to eye. For some reason, I find you very attractive and I'm drawn to the person you are. But it seems I need to break it off with you completely."

"Do I have a say in this matter?" Kelly put her hands on her hips. "You always change your mind and come to me. I know you've had more than your share of broken relationships. But honey, I understand. That's why I'm here."

"You don't know what this girl means to me. I don't want Shandele or anybody nosing around in my personal affairs."

"I know you dated Shandele, too."

"It wasn't a date. It was dinner because I ran into her at a sushi restaurant. We were both dining alone."

"Ah, but you remember it. You sweet-talked her."

"Until I found out she was engaged. She should have told me that from the beginning."

"You don't see it, do you? You're a main attraction. You're needy too. I don't believe this is the end because you'll never change."

"All I'm asking is for a little consideration in the workplace. I don't want gossip or people criticizing my actions. Tell Shandele to lay off."

Kelly stood back and picked up her empty coffee cup and threw it in the wastebasket. "The world doesn't revolve around you but you think the sun sets on your side of the fence." She stomped out.

Blair felt tense after speaking to Kelly. He wondered if she was right. Was Jennifer the right one or was he going to fall into old patterns again? He needed to talk so he called his sister Jeanne.

"Hey, Jeanne. How are you?"

Jeanne picked up the phone at her office. She worked in payroll for a department store chain. "What's up, Blair? Aren't you at the bank? Must be important or are you trying to sell me an RRSP?"

"I'm not calling to discuss registered retirement savings plan options. Actually I'm having problems at work."

"Are you kidding me? Everyone has problems especially in the workplace."

"Do you remember meeting Kelly? Well, I'm not going to see her anymore," said Blair.

"How could I forget a woman like that? You need to find someone to date outside the office."

"How do you forgive yourself for being a heel?"

Jeanne laughed. "Are we talking about you? Because I don't think we're talking about me."

"I'm just saying things are different since I met Jen."

"Oh, you're calling her by a nickname now. Must be on familiar terms. Are you seeing her regularly?" Jeanne asked in an amused tone.

"Cut it out. I'm still waiting for the right time."

"What's the hold-up?"

"Red tape," he said.

"So what? Work around the problem. I've never seen you this hyped up about anyone."

"I'm a little afraid of her not liking me or my job or something," Blair said.

"Your idiosyncrasies are endearing qualities in a man. Having confidence is all right nowadays. Did you hear about that?"

"Jen leaves me a little tongue-tied. I called Sean Abrams one day and she answered. I didn't know what to say. I couldn't concentrate for the rest of the call."

"Is this infatuation or is this falling for real?" said Jeanne.

"She's exceptional. Very gifted. Sean says she can do anything."

"I thought you said she doesn't even work full-time anymore. I appreciate the fact Sean loves his daughter but she's only human."

"Sean says she's had setbacks, but he truly believes in her."

"Is she going to fit into your world?" Jeanne asked. "What do you have in common?"

"I don't know yet. I hope we're going to get along."

"Do you hear what you are saying? You're planning on something, building castles in the air about a relationship you don't have yet."

"The timing has to be right. We need time to get to know each other. She's only twenty-six."

"She's young. Is she going to want a family?"

"I've started to think about kids."

"So why don't you ask her out?" said Jeanne.

Blair called Sean on Jennifer's day off. "Sean, when is the time going to be right to ask out Jen?"

Sean turned his chair to look out the window at the twelve-storey building that housed the bank. He visualized Blair in his office. "I told you before, you have to wait. The government has the right to veto your involvement before it even begins. It's for the sake of the research study. Ideally, we'd like her to be well and off medication before she leaves her family and lives with or marries someone else."

"So it may be awhile. Will she recover for sure?"

"We don't know. But we are hoping for the best. The people involved are under pressure to find a cure. She's made a lot of headway. We think she's close to the end of her illness. Sometimes these things burn out. That's the prognosis and I agree. Just sit back and relax. You're our first choice."

Blair took a long breath. "That's reassuring. But what if she never recovers?"

"Then we try it another way."

"She called me and left a message, but I didn't call her back."

"Be patient." Sean said goodbye and went back to his daily business.

Chapter 7

Dr. Hutchinson was reviewing an audio tape of an interview with Jennifer Abrams recorded when she was sixteen. Dr. Camen listened to the tape with him. Her voice came across clear and strong, as did her message.

"I don't want my suffering to be for nothing." Jennifer's voice was determined. "I want to aid in finding a cure even to my own detriment. I think this is a golden opportunity. I can give you insight into the psychological aspects of mental illness. I have ideas to aid the mentally ill and to streamline public mental health services. I only ask in return that I will always be taken care of, no matter what."

A male voice asked, "What could you suggest regarding public mental health services?"

"Your emergency rooms and psychiatric units are overextended. I think you need a 24/7 centralized hotline for people to receive care for mental health problems. The hotline should connect them with access to the right service or field questions to avoid clogging up emergency services. Also, you need to improve mental health housing and community mental health services. Community-based services keep people well for less funding versus the cost of acute care. You need more generic-approved medications to bring down costs. In order to find a cure, you can run mental stress tests on me to see how I perform under pressure. I believe I will recover. Study my progress."

"Do you understand what you are offering? Can you handle additional pressure?" the male voice asked.

"I'm resilient. I handled hearing voices for nine months. I know myself. Just study me," Jennifer said adamantly.

He pressed the stop button and turned to Dr. Camen. "That's the original recording of an interview during her first stay in hospital under psychiatric care."

Dr. Camen said, "Inspiring to say the least. How is she doing recently?"

"We have evidence that supports recovery. She has partial

recovery at this time. She has fewer symptoms, less withdrawal, no more evidence of depression, better coping strategies. And most importantly, she's taking care of herself."

"Self-care. The strategy we want to enforce in all our clients. How is her self-esteem? Is she still highly self-critical?"

"That's the crux of it. I believe her grandiose delusions and fantasies are a symptom of low self-esteem levels. When unwell, she not only believes she's a creative genius, but a clairvoyant with a photographic memory. She must develop self-confidence on her own. No one can do it for her. It's a slow process because she herself discourages feelings of self-worth."

"What does she need to cross the line into a sense of well-being? What's the time frame?"

"I'm not sure. At least a year."

"If that's what it takes, so be it. A year isn't that far off. I'll study her current interview tapes and give my analysis to the board." They shook hands and Dr. Camen left the office.

Some viewed Dr. Hutchinson as a hard-liner, but he was effective, well respected and knowledgeable. Aloofness protected him from succumbing to stress on the job and taking on the problems of his clients.

When Jennifer was twenty-three, he had tried to cure Jennifer by coercion upon her own request. Around that time, she came into a meeting and flat out told him, she wanted to try to burn the illness out of her. She said, "I'm not getting any better. It's frustrating. I need you to push me to the limit. Create the most stressful environment you can. Drop me over the edge until the chemical imbalance in my brain burns itself out. Because the way it's working now, I'm not getting anywhere."

He changed the topic. "How are you sleeping these days? Perhaps we should raise your medication to help you sleep."

"Did you hear what I said? Tell me, is it a good idea?"

Dr. Hutchinson shifted in his chair and directed his gaze to the picture, hanging on the wall behind her. It was a lithograph of a seascape. He looked back at her. She leaned forward on the edge of her seat, waiting for a response.

"How's your appetite?" he asked.

"You don't hear me, do you?" She folded her arms and looked at the carpet. She rocked back and forth, looking distracted.

"So your appetite is fine?"

"How can you sit there and not hear me? I know you are experimenting on me. I know I'm a research subject. So let's just cut the act and discuss reality. If my symptoms are caused by a chemical imbalance, if my brain was over-stimulated, there's a chance all the junk would blow out and I'd be sane again. That's what I want. Isn't that what you want?"

"At the team, we are behind you." Dr. Hutchinson remained elusive.

"Then can't you help me?"

"Illness doesn't just evaporate. What you have is chronic." Dr. Hutchinson looked at the seascape picture again. He avoided looking her in the eye. "Schizophrenia isn't something you can just cure overnight." He didn't want to give her any hint of advantage or control over the meeting.

After she left, he reflected on her ability to shift from typical schizophrenic patient to illness expert. She could think on different levels with a flip of a hat. Her amnesia made it possible for her to change quickly.

She led a dual existence. Sometimes she was alert and high functioning; other times she would have extreme lows. She bordered on having a dual personality but she could aid the research, which was a more important issue in his eyes.

After discussing Jennifer's request with several other specialists on the team, Dr. Hutchinson put the go ahead on creating a paranoid environment for Jennifer. Dr. Hutchinson was in charge of monitoring her progress and adjusting her medications. Secretly, someone contacted someone to let the air out of her car tires in underground parking. Someone contacted Sean Abrams to move her purse secretly from one locker to another at work. A man spied on her openly for four hours. As a result of these stresses over the period of three weeks, she became very ill. She arrived at the next meeting fearful and anxious.

"I can't understand the bad luck I've been having. I'm making errors at work. I can't concentrate. I feel there's a conspiracy against me."

Dr. Hutchinson said, "Increase your medication by five milligrams. I'll see you next week." He raised her medication to insure she didn't go over the edge any further.

Jennifer left the meeting perplexed and confused. Dr. Hutchinson had cut her short. She didn't have the opportunity to discuss details of the events that were bothering her. Surely, her psychiatrist couldn't and wouldn't tell someone to let air out of her car's tires or spy on her. She had no proof that there was a conspiracy against her. She tried to force herself to see the wrongful events as unrelated.

On the one hand, she vaguely recalled the conversation she had with Dr. Hutchinson about burning the illness out of her system; but on the other, he gave no evidence that these events were anything more than bad luck. She doubted her own memory. Wasn't it unethical for him to psychologically harm her regardless? He avoided answering her accusations. She grew more suspicious. It was like being on a rollercoaster she couldn't get off.

Dr. Hutchinson had his own agenda. Raising her dosage levels would make her functioning more difficult especially at work. He wanted to push her hard.

She came in the next week to see him.

"Dr. Hutchinson, I can't believe you'd do this to me!" She was defensive. "I'm going to lose my job! Please forget what I said. I just want to feel normal again. The whole world is against me." She spoke in a rage and broke into tears during the session.

"At work, I flared up. I accused a co-worker of going through my desk. My papers had been moved. My calculator was gone. My father walked in and told me to leave the office at once. I feel the world is caving in! Call off the dogs!" She pounded the arms of her chair with her fists.

Dr. Hutchinson knew she was tough, really tough with the energy of a twenty-three-year-old. She was responding to the stresses with aggression, suspicion and anger. He ordered her to drop her present medication to nil in two days and introduced a new replacement drug. He knew the abrupt changes in medication were severe. It would put her over the edge as she intended.

Dr. Hutchinson met with several others on the team. He said, "Jennifer is so angry and paranoid she can hardly function at work. She's also developed physical symptoms such as a respiratory problem and chronic back pain. Her tolerance level is extremely low."

"Despite your tactics, I see what she's trying to do with your help. But I stand opposed on moral grounds," said one of the group.

"What's your next step?" asked another.

"Hospitalization and a full analysis by hospital staff," said Dr. Hutchinson. "I need an independent assessment."

Accidentally, Jennifer cut herself with sewing scissors in her drawer. She developed delusional thinking. She spent most of her time curled up in bed, staring at the wall. She'd missed a week of work. Her mother said, "Dad and I think you need to go into hospital for awhile. You aren't well, Jen."

She was admitted to a hospital psychiatric ward, based on the possibility that she might harm herself. She had a series of blood tests, and various brain scans. Her blood pressure was high. The doctors and other medical staff watched her closely. She displayed odd behaviours like scratching her arms and pulling at her hair.

After two months, she was able to leave hospital. She was stabilizing on her new medication. Relatively, she was calmer and more aware of her surroundings. She was relieved when her mother picked her up, but was silent on the drive home.

Dr. Hutchinson received the final release report, but he couldn't discern if the extreme stress cured her. It was too early to tell.

To Sean, she voiced that she missed work and wanted her old routine back at the office. She came in for an hour at a time to do simple duties on a volunteer basis. She was still in recovery and would make a number of errors in her typing. Sean told the other staff members to check her work and correct her mistakes. Jennifer tried as hard as she could to do her job as she had before.

Slowly, she improved based on determination and perseverance. Sean recognized her efforts and paid her an honorarium.

Sean called Dr. Hutchinson for a progress report. "What's the diagnosis now?"

"She's fair. Her symptoms are decreasing, but it's going to take awhile."

"But did our little conspiracy work? Did the paranoid environment flush it out of her?" Sean asked.

"She is still in need of medication, but overall I'd say she is better than before. There are serious consequences and other implications if this type of coercion works on mentally ill patients."

"It's a far cry from electric shock treatment," replied Sean.

"The mind is one of the most complex areas of scientific study. What works for some with mental illness, doesn't work for others."

"Is she still angry at you?" asked Sean.

"She's uncomfortable in meetings, but she doesn't want to switch to another psychiatrist at this point. Besides, there's a six-month waiting list to find another one. The study will continue despite whoever treats her. I wanted to ask you, where does she get her strength to bounce back after such a nasty setback? Two months ago she couldn't leave the house. Now she's started jogging in the mornings. She's unstoppable."

Sean smiled proudly. "She's my only one."

"You're the same, aren't you?"

"The apple doesn't fall far from the tree."

Sean ended the call.

Dr. Hutchinson appreciated Jennifer's willpower. She had spent years dedicating herself to the cause. She had a mental illness and a history of bad luck she couldn't shake. Yet despite those odds, she still persevered. Her recovery was something to be proud of, not just for her but for every person in the psychiatric sphere, because if she could be healed under these circumstances, there was hope for other mentally ill people. She contributed so much to society while remaining the same, unique, humble person. Her accomplishments despite adversity were beyond expectation. He also knew she had no inkling she was important or special, no reason to believe she would benefit financially from this study nor proof it even existed. They covered their tracks well. Anything out of the ordinary was labeled as part of her psychosis.

In her own words, her reward was to be taken care of, to have enough money—not an extravagant amount—just enough. How do you reward someone for such an enormous commitment? Sean had something to say about that.

Sean said to Charles and Blair over lunch, "All successes are relative. The first case I ever won was more significant to me than most of the ones I've had since. I wasn't paid that much for it and it wasn't a big case, but it was my first one. Jennifer, as any of us, would like recognition and rewards for her efforts, but she lives her life based on her own formula, her own need to be purposeful and all-inclusive. She wants acceptance and to live her life the way it was meant for her."

Sean Abrams was man of logic. Every decision he made was based on weighing the pros and cons, methodically without emotional reasons. When Jennifer was very young, they knew she was above average in intelligence. But they did not allow her to skip grades because her maturity level and social development were below average. She saw herself as an ordinary little girl. She was a happy child and enjoyed summer vacation with her parents at the cottage by the lake. When Jennifer became ill, he and his wife's decision to allow their daughter to be studied was not an easy one. At that time, he decided to put it before the courts to decide if it was legal.

The Provincial Court judge heard Sean's argument and quickly denied his proposal, citing it illegal, unethical and preposterous. The case was appealed in the BC Supreme Court where the proposal was again refused. Sean's final chance was the Court of Appeal.

Sean rehearsed his argument carefully. He stood before three judges and began, "Jennifer Abrams is a significant individual. Do not let her age of sixteen fool you. She is astute, more focused than most. She is an independent thinker and gifted. She is giving us an opportunity to evaluate her progress, to use her instincts and insights to improve our knowledge of mental illness and improve services. She is not asking a lot, but giving us what we need. As parents, we support the work. Certainly, it is for the common good to proceed with the research."

One of the judges asked, "Is it possible the study will be detrimental to her?"

"I'm not a doctor, a psychologist or a psychiatrist. But I know legally if all sides agree, there is no wrongdoing."

"Legally it can be done, but I question the ethics. The procedure isn't foolproof," the judge said.

"If working for the common good is ethical, then it is ethical," Sean responded. "The proposal is to observe her in an environmental study. Health professionals will run blood tests, MRIs and any other tests that are necessary. The results will be used to analyze hematological and brain abnormalities and to search for new medicines to treat schizophrenia. She will be treated by the best psychiatrists in the city. Any drugs prescribed for her will be approved by Health Canada. In return, she will receive the best possible care as we search for a cure."

Sean's arguments and self-assurance impressed the judges, but they knew as well as anyone that to use a human as a guinea pig was unethical. As a minor, she could not make this decision legally. However, they knew there was a way to get around it. Behind closed doors, it was decided Mr. and Mrs. Abrams would not take the responsibility of the court's decision for their child. Instead, the child in question would be signed over as a ward of the state and that would alleviate Mr. and Mrs. Abrams of any illegal consequence. The government would make medical and legal decisions on Jennifer's behalf. Jennifer would remain in her parents' home, but only as their charge. The governing body would perceive Jennifer as a classified human subject labeled anonymously as "Madame J." Sean honestly felt he was doing the right thing. He knew his daughter was selfless and believed in her. If anyone could do it, it would be she.

However, Sean's projections for his daughter went beyond the time limitations of the study. He wanted to be assured she would have everything she needed in the future. In his opinion, she needed the protection and love of a husband and the benefits of a career. He knew she could not survive alone; she needed a mate. He asked the government for assurance that she would not commit suicide or harm herself in any way and be protected from physical harm from others. Even with the best of care, Jennifer could possibly attempt to take her own life. She needed to be watched at all times. So the government set up 24-hour surveillance to tail Madame J.

Sean set up an insurance policy that if Jennifer were to die prematurely, he and his wife would receive one million dollars for pain and suffering and to close her affairs. Sean felt guilt to a degree but after assessing the situation, he felt Jennifer was the person to decide her own fate not him, even at the age of sixteen. She knew the consequences as well as anyone. By cooperating with the government and researchers, he would also be part of the quest for a better world.

Also Sean kept abreast of the progress of the study. Research into brain chemistry made many advances and discoveries during the years Jennifer participated in the study. Besides MRIs, CT scans and blood tests, she had intelligence and psychological tests. They measured her growth patterns to see if the medication affected her physical development. They made sure she had a good diet, enough exercise and sleep. They watched her behaviour closely and wrote reports meticulously about her actions, attitudes, likes and dislikes. They knew what type of things made her happy and what made her sad. They knew her weaknesses and her strengths. And they found out what her parents already knew. She was really special.

Mrs. Abrams was silent through most of the process. She put all her faith in her husband's decisions, believing he would do the right thing. She knew that despite Jennifer's perceptiveness, she could not avoid the pain and suffering she endured as a mentally ill person. She really went through hell when she became psychotic or suicidal, and her family suffered with her. Mrs. Abrams did all she could to comfort her. Jennifer's behaviour could be erratic, but underneath, Mrs. Abrams knew Jennifer was still her daughter that she raised and loved. She prayed that Jennifer would not suffer greatly, but would find peace within herself and be happy and content in the future. She felt God would not allow Jennifer more suffering than she could handle.

Chapter 8

Blair was sleeping in Sunday morning when the phone rang. He answered it after three rings.

"Is that Blair?" came a voice over the line. "It's Bill."

"Bill who?" Blair yawned and looked at the clock. It was 10 a.m.

"I'm on Jennifer's list. I'm calling long distance from Australia."

Blair was suddenly alert. "Well, how did you get this number?"

"Robbie gave it to me."

"Of course, I should have known."

Bill said, "I want to tell you something. You don't know what she's like. She will lead you on so long and then she'll dump you. All she wants is to manipulate you."

Blair rubbed his temples. He was mildly curious about Bill's motive in calling him.

Bill rattled on. "She's a big headache. She's no good for anybody."

"I can see why you're back on the list." Blair wondered if his sarcasm would be lost on Bill.

"I told my fiancée Emma, I only want Jennifer for the money. We're postponing our wedding for now until I can find work."

"Oh, that's smart." Blair thought what a major mistake it would be if Jennifer chose Bill.

"You don't know what you are getting into. Robbie says she can be very unstable at times, get angry or paranoid and treat you badly."

"Robbie doesn't know what he's talking about. Neither do you, for that matter. I'm guessing these statements are not based on firsthand experience."

"She's mentally ill! Don't you understand?" Bill was shouting now.

"Bill, take it easy. You're not thinking straight. If you don't like her, drop your name from the list. Other than that, I have no reason to continue this conversation."

"You're wrong and you know you're wrong."

"Sounds like sour grapes to me and the contest hasn't begun yet."

"You're in for a rough ride," snarled Bill.

Disgusted, Blair ended the call. He didn't like competing with the others. He was better than this.

Blair received a call from Jeanne after noon. A golf tournament was on television. He stretched from the sofa to the phone when it rang. Behind him, boxes of his belongings filled the dining room ready for the move. It was going to be soon.

"Hey, Blair. Want to come to dinner? I'm inviting Elaine, you know the fashion photographer I told you about? She really wants to meet you."

Blair answered. "Sorry, I have a girlfriend."

"Are you talking about Jennifer? You haven't even dated her. Are you saying you don't want to meet Elaine? She's your type. Live a little," Jeanne said.

"I'm not biting."

"Tell me again why this girl is so important to you."

"Did I tell you about the time she was in the teller line-up one time and I stood by her and coughed?"

"What did she do? Cough back?" Jeanne was amused.

"No, she turned to me and said, 'Excuse me, are you the bank manager?' I was speechless. I mean, no one would mistake me for the manager of the bank. I felt flattered."

"And then what happened?" Jeanne asked.

"She said, 'Do you think the bank could offer free coffee first thing in the morning? That would be a good idea.' Then a teller opened up and she left me standing there."

"So is there free coffee at your bank now?"

"I suggested it, and the bank did set up a percolator for about three weeks."

"Did it attract customers?" Jeanne said.

"At first it was a hit, but then the manager decided it wasn't necessary."

"So it was a good idea, but it didn't pan out. She's a thinker, isn't she?"

"Sometimes she manages the phones at Abrams and Co. She has a great telephone manner."

"You really like her. I can tell. I can't wait to meet her."

"Honest?"

"Honest," said Jeanne.

Jennifer started to submit to various poetry journals and fiction magazines. She wanted to break into the writers' market. Out of her first ten submissions, only one was accepted. She made a grand total of twenty-five dollars. This is really tough, she thought to herself. Maybe I'm not such a good writer. She was conflicted and discouraged. Other writers that she met on chat groups online had told her they received many rejection letters before their work was accepted. It took years to become a writer. Somewhere inside of her, she really believed in her writing. She imagined the people in charge were holding her back. Perhaps because of the conspiracy, they were preventing her from having success.

Dr. Hutchinson knew their plan was so complicated; it would be virtually impossible for her to figure out the truth. He surmised she would recover almost immediately, if given the recognition and success she deserved and needed. By cutting back her chances of success, he knew she would have difficulties internally and externally. He wanted to know what made her different. What made Jennifer keep trying day after day? Her desire for self-preservation made her a fighter. He spent long hours trying to keep ahead of her. If she came into a meeting discussing her fears, he made sure to use them against her. As smart as she was, she had to deal with the circumstances placed before her.

Sean also tried to keep a step ahead of Jennifer.

"Dad." Jennifer poked her head in the door of his office. He had a lot of rosewood in his office giving it a refined appearance.

"That's Mr. Abrams to you." He narrowed his eyes for effect.

She smiled. "Just looking over your phone log. What are these calls to Blair Whitman? I didn't know he was a client." She paged through the log casually looking at the entries.

Sean stood up and took the log from her. "It's business. Leave it alone. When were you elected to oversee my affairs?"

"Oh, I'm sorry. I didn't mean anything by it. I'm curious. Is he wanted on embezzlement charges?"

"None of your business. Get back to work." She turned to walk away then stopped.

"Someone at the mental health team called. Anything I should know about?"

"Probably a wrong number. Get busy."

She nodded and closed the door behind her. Sean glanced at the phone log on his desk. A little too close for comfort, he thought. He decided as of then, no private calls from the office phone.

"Hi," James answered his cellphone as he pushed a button to call an elevator. He had an appointment on the fifth floor.

"It's Robbie. Did you know I have you on speed dial?"

"What do you want?"

"Have you seen Jennifer recently?"

"Actually, no. I haven't."

"Blair is the first one. Then comes Mark. Then you." Robbie reminded him.

The elevator doors opened. James pressed the button for the fifth floor. He was the only passenger as the elevator lifted. "You told me this already."

"She's really sophisticated. Needs everything provided for her. It's going to cost bucks to take care of her. You're out of your league."

"So what? If I have a chance maybe I can make something of it. Besides, she's rich enough to support me by the sounds of it." James felt the elevator rise.

"Do you know she's twenty-six? You're what? Seventeen?"

"You know I'm nineteen. Her age doesn't bother me." The elevator doors opened and James walked into the corridor and turned left.

"Are you going to be able to keep her loyal?" Robbie taunted.

"Why do you keep calling me? Don't you have anything

better to do?"

"I told you I'm trying to dissuade you up because I don't want you to go to bed with her," Robbie said.

"I'm ahead of you. You have to wait six weeks after I make contact and that's only if you are reinstated," James said.

"Once you got back in, I realized I wanted back in too. I was reinstated on Thursday. This isn't just a game. It could change my life. I've been in love with her for years. This is a biggie for me. I need her more than you can imagine."

"You're a clown."

"Look, if you've got a chance, then I have one, too. Appearance-wise, we're similar, you and I. You're younger but I'm wiser."

"Look, I got to go. I'm meeting my psychiatrist."

"What's his name?" Robbie said.

"None of your business." James replied. He clicked off his cellphone.

James entered the mental health team and spoke to the receptionist. Minutes later, James's case manager greeted him and led him down the hallway to Dr. Maine's office. She knocked and opened the door.

"Our four o'clock, Dr. Maine," she said. James swaggered in. The case manager closed the door and sat down with a pen and pad.

Dr. Maine said hello as James took a seat. "Tell me how the last few weeks have been for you?"

"Robbie keeps harassing me on the phone."

"I warned you about participating in this contest. You may come out disappointed. I'd gladly see you in a meaningful relationship, but I think this person may not be the right one for you."

"I'm an adult who can make his own decisions. You deal with my mental health, but my social life is my business."

"This woman goes deep with you? I know you said you feel something, but maybe you should wait until you are more stable," cautioned Dr. Maine.

"I'm stable enough to rent my own place, stay out of hospital and hold down a part-time job. What else do you want?" James leaned back in his chair.

Dr. Maine leaned forward. "Do you need to take care of this Robbie? Do you need to block his calls?"

"I already tried that, but he texted me or posted things on Facebook. So we agreed I would unblock his calls if he didn't post things about me on Facebook. He calls day or night. He wants a chance with her. He tries to appeal to my sense of fair play. He's hyped up when he calls me."

"Why talk to him at all?"

"Curiosity. It boggles my mind how he can be so in love with her and have had no real contact with her. The more I hear from Robbie, the more I want her. By my calculation, it's going to take at least eight months for her to go through everybody. It's wild."

Dr. Maine said, "Consider finding a girlfriend closer to your age in your circle."

"Is that an order? Because I don't take orders."

"It's only a suggestion," Dr. Maine said. "You've made remarkable progress on the right medication since being diagnosed eighteen months ago. You're self-reliant, capable and sensible. I don't want you getting hurt caught up in a fiasco."

They continued their conversation behind closed doors.

One day at the law office, Sean got an unexpected call on his private line.

"Hello, Sean. It's Dr. Hutchinson. I have been meaning to call you about your daughter."

Sean was curious. It was very rare Dr. Hutchinson would call him. Sean hoped Jennifer wouldn't walk in on the call.

"I want to tell you that Blair has tough decisions to make. He has very little knowledge about mental illness. Two of the others have mental illnesses themselves that gives them more understanding of ways to help her cope. Is Jennifer really going to fit into Blair's world?"

"Are you saying he's the wrong one?" Sean asked.

"I'm not saying that. I'm just making you aware that there may be a different outcome than what you expect. There's a lot of benefit to be had, if Jennifer picks someone who can encourage her creativity. Perhaps it's not about the order. It's about who's the best."

"Or whom she falls for first?" asked Sean.

"We want her to experience love."

Sean said, "She's had casual boyfriends in the past. She's not too wise about men."

"Have you heard about James? He's an independent thinker. Street smarts. Charisma. Once the ball starts rolling, it'll be out of our hands," warned Dr. Hutchinson.

"I can see that. Can I ask you something?"

"Certainly," said Dr. Hutchinson.

"How much are you getting to review and process in this project?"

Dr. Hutchinson was silent.

"Are you getting as much money as she's getting? What's your motivation?"

Dr. Hutchinson said, "I get what I've always gotten. Twenty-five percent above the second highest government paid psychiatrist in the province."

"And what kind of perks are you getting?" Sean asked. "An expense account? A discretionary fund in order to produce a dilemma in her?"

"I'm not under oath here, nor do I have to answer this line of questioning."

"I want to understand that you have her best interest at heart."

"I would think twice about laying judgment. How about you, Sean? She's your daughter. Believe me, for what we are doing as a team, no one gets off scot-free. We are all faced with the moral dilemma wrapped up in technicality. No one is above the law."

"You still feel guilt? I got over that a long time ago."

"You're the lucky one." Dr. Hutchinson ended the call.

Chapter 9

Blair met Chad Tyson, his university buddy, at a bar on Robson Street. Blair loosened up on account of the beer. "No one has six people they could love equally. I think there's a statute of limitations on that," he said.

Chad said, "What's this girl to you, anyway?"

"I don't know how to describe it. I'm not after her for her money. Her father says he wants to aid us financially, but if he pays, that puts my role in question. It's about self-respect. How can I look in the mirror if I feel I'm being bought?"

"What about the money she's already earned?"

"She can keep it."

"The government has no right to prevent you from doing anything. It's just dating, for god's sake."

"I'm not going to be badgered anymore or chained to a set of rules," said Blair.

Chad said, "Now that's the Blair Whitman I know! Go with your instincts. They're always right."

Jennifer was trying on an old pair of jeans and couldn't do up the zipper. She wondered if she had gained weight. She stepped on the bathroom scale and found she had put on ten pounds since last year. She decided to measure her height against the marks on the bathroom doorframe. Her parents had recorded her height over the years with pencil marks and dates. Surprised, she found she had gained an inch.

How could she have grown that much recently? She was well past the normal growth stage. Was she standing straighter? Then she started to think. For the past six months, she'd been experiencing back pain, knee pain and muscle tightness. What had caused this? Then she thought perhaps the medication she was taking for mental illness was causing her to grow. Was it some kind of growth hormone or derivative? If it activated her pituitary gland, could she become taller? She investigated her theory by accessing information on the internet. She couldn't find much information and there was no direct evidence that her medication was affecting her height. She decided a wait-and-see approach was best and went back to her daily activities.

At one time, Blair was the unsung hero of bachelor dating. He experienced a lot of relationships with different women. He had a set of dating rules. For example, he never slept with a woman on the first date unless she was very sensual and made overtures. If sex didn't happen by the third date, most of the women started to wonder if they weren't attractive enough and would call and ask him out instead. He didn't always carry condoms; some women carried their own. He never fell for a woman in a big way. To him, women were basically the same. They liked to be coddled, flattered and date good-looking men with money or the potential to get it. Dollar signs lit up their eyes. His charm and polite attitude impressed women. Little did they know, he wasn't for sale. He never loved anyone enough to get engaged or married previously. He lived with one woman for six years. She left him for someone else. Now she was married with two children.

Would Jennifer have held his interest if it wasn't for Sean's persistent calls and conversations? With so many intriguing circumstances, he felt drawn to her but he hadn't spent much time one-on-one.

He didn't have a problem approaching her like Robbie did. He wasn't in Australia like Bill. Or have a carrot top like Chris who was afraid to even enter a room. He wasn't a young stud like James, but he wasn't mentally ill either. He thought about Mark. He was the closest competitor to him according to height. But why would Jennifer consider all these different men? Romance with any one of the six would result in very different outcomes. Despite his financial status and career, he realized he might not be the right mate for Jennifer. Money wasn't really a deciding factor in her choice if she had her own wealth. And he liked his freedom to do as he pleased. The only way he'd find out if she were the right choice was to spend time with her.

On impulse, he grabbed his phone and punched Jennifer's number. The waiting game was over. It was time for his next move.

Jennifer answered. "Hello?"

"Hi, Jen. It's me, Blair Whitman."

"Hello, I just stepped out of the shower."

Blair pictured her stepping out of the shower and towel-drying her hair with the morning sun shining through her bedroom window.

"Are you calling about a painting?" Jennifer said.

"Actually no. I would like to ask you for dinner Saturday if you don't have plans."

She leaned back on her bed. "What brings this about?"

"I want to get to know you."

"What do you need to know about me? Is there a quiz involved?"

"You are being a little hard on me, wouldn't you say? I know this bistro on tenth. Interested? How 'bout I pick you up around seven?"

"Sounds terrific."

"Great. See you then." Blair hung up the phone.

Blair wondered if he was doing the right thing. To hell with the system, he thought. Rules were made to be broken. Life was too short to run around in circles waiting for the door to open.

Saturday evening, Blair arrived at the Abrams' residence. He rang the bell. Mrs. Abrams answered with a smile and called upstairs for Jennifer. She came down the steps wearing a chocolate knit dress and an ivory satin jacket. He was surprised she was so dressed so elegantly. She took one look at his cotton twill pants and said, "Maybe I should change."

"No, you look great," he said. She looked radiant. He waved goodbye to Mrs. Abrams and led her down the front walk to his car.

Blair glanced at her sideways with a puzzled look.

"Is something the matter?" she asked with her hand on the car door. He opened it for her.

"You look taller somehow, or maybe it's my imagination."

"I would say it's the high heels, but the truth is I've grown an inch in the last six months."

"Aren't you a little old for that or am I robbing the cradle?"

She smiled and slid into the passenger seat. "As a matter of fact, I thought you were a little old for me."

"I'm not in a wheelchair yet." He shut the car door and got in the driver's seat.

"While, we're on the subject, how old are you?" she asked.

"I'll tell you when it won't matter anymore."

"You mean I'm going to see you again after tonight?"

He didn't answer the question, just put the car in drive and headed for the bistro.

They sat outside under a patio umbrella. A waitress brought them menus. It was unusually warm.

Jennifer looked at the menu. "I think I'm going to have the king crab."

"Of course, you choose the most expensive thing on the menu. What is it about women anyway? They starve all week so they can eat out on the weekends," said Blair.

"There aren't any prices on this menu. How am I supposed to make a choice based on the prices?" She frowned. "Can I order a peanut butter sandwich with a glass of milk or is that out of your budget?"

"Take it easy. I'm not going to tell you what not to order. Sure, have the king crab."

"I changed my mind. I'd like the strawberry spinach salad and salmon with rice pilaf." Jennifer closed her menu.

A waitress appeared and took their order. Blair asked for a glass of wine. Jennifer sipped from her water glass.

Blair leaned back. "So you went from ordering the thirty-dollar king crab legs to ordering a twelve-dollar item with a free glass of water."

"I find your comments excruciating. What's with you bankers always concerned about money?"

Blair smiled. "I'm just making conversation."

"How do you know the prices? They weren't listed."

"Because I've eaten here many times, but not with anyone as beautiful as you."

Across the street, Robbie crouched behind a bus stop shelter. He held a pair of binoculars. He had a sound amplifier, aimed at them to hear their conversation. It angered him to see Jennifer with Blair. They didn't have anything in common. Blair was all about money and business; Jennifer was an artist. He noted how she played with her hair, crossed her legs and made circles with the toe of her sandal. This was too much. Blair was way too old school for her.

By chance, James came walking the street. He spotted Robbie. He walked over, flicked his cigarette and said, "What the hell are you doing?"

"James, get down," whispered Robbie. "What the hell are you doing here?"

"Just out strolling, my friend."

"Watch out. She'll see us." He pointed across the street at the pair dining at the bistro.

James kneeled beside him and broke out with laughter. "I don't believe you are actually spying on her date. Don't you have anything else to do?"

"Be quiet. He's holding her hand."

"Let me see your binoculars. Wow, you've even got earphones!"

Robbie passed James the binoculars and one earphone so they both could hear. "Don't let them see you."

James looked through the lenses for a close-up view. Robbie gaped as Blair moved his chair closer to Jennifer and reached out his hand to touch hers. "You know you're really something," Blair said to Jennifer. His voice was loud and clear through the earphones.

James said, "Good god. He's really a poet, isn't he?"

Robbie said, "I can't hear them talking. Would you shut up?"

"They're talking about you, actually."

Robbie said, "Very funny. Give those back." He took the binoculars and earphone back from James.

"I saw her at the mental health team not five days ago," said James.

"Your point being?" Robbie untangled the cord to the earphones.

"She looked at me and curled her tongue. I used to think she was shy, but now she flirts more. What's the chance of me calling her on Blair's cell and I take her to dinner?" James looked amused.

Blair smiled at Jennifer who had started on her strawberry and spinach salad.

"This salad dressing is delicious!" Jennifer exclaimed.

The waitress served Blair a plate of fettuccini Alfredo.

James said, "I tell you. She's ripe. Man, Blair's the slowest make-out artist I've ever seen. Just jump her!"

Robbie was silent, listening to the couple's conversation. They talked about their favourite vacation spots. Blair said, "I enjoyed the Mediterranean. The cruise was the highlight of my trip."

Jennifer smiled at him as if he'd just bought her a five thousand dollar ring. She admired him like a peasant honouring the Pope.

James stood up. "I find this embarrassing to sneak around spying on people. It's a new low for me. Is it a habit of yours? My advice to you is to stop spying on people and live your own life."

After dinner, Robbie followed Blair and Jennifer to the beach. He parked a distance away. The wind rustled through the trees. Seagulls cawed high above them. The sun set low in the sky. It was a romantic evening. Blair held her hand as they walked along a sandy path. Robbie decided he had enough and left.

Blair took her home by ten and stood on her porch. Standing on her tiptoes, she kissed him good night. He left with a wave and honked his horn as he drove off. He knew Sean would be watching his every move, so he didn't want to blow it. He thought about his next step. He wanted to go as slow as possible, make it interesting. Once his six week advantage was over, he'd be competing against Mark. He thought Mark was an okay guy, but he had to be eliminated from the race along with the others. How trustworthy was she so early in the relationship? Warning bells went off in his head.

The following week, Blair was at the diner when Sean came down for lunch.

"May I join you?" Sean asked. Blair nodded. "I hear you had an evening out with Jennifer."

"Ah, you found me out." Blair placed a napkin in his lap. A waitress brought him a clubhouse sandwich. Sean ordered the same.

"Is there a problem that I jumped the gun?" asked Blair.

"Not really. It's doable. I realize I'm a little overprotective. Life is to be lived in freedom, not under the thumb of strict government control. We welcomed you into the inner circle and we feel your honesty speaks to your character. Your actions from this point on will be considered independent. We don't want to chain you to obligation or interfere in your relationship with Jennifer."

"Good. I thought they'd come after me. Did she say anything to you about how it went?" asked Blair.

"No, but my wife said she had a good time. I have something to say."

"What is it?"

"I've been talking to Dr. Hutchinson and I believe another may have an equal chance."

"I thought you were behind me."

"Well, there are things I found out about James," stressed Sean.

Blair was getting riled. "What about James?"

"He's an artist. He's had it rough. He has a mental health issue like her. He's experienced a lot in his life. He's unpretentious. Very bright, actually."

Blair rapped his knuckles on the table. "He's too young, perhaps?"

"No more than you are older than she."

"I'm not into playing games. I'm into winning. Is this just some big joke? I mean it's beyond me the way this is going to play out. The other candidates aren't people in my circle. They are a bunch of young studs. I refuse to be put in a position of trying to keep tabs on her, making sure that she isn't out with anyone of them. I have a certain standard of what I want in a relationship and the type of woman I want. Is she going to have lunch and entertain each of these guys on my time?"

Sean said, "Relax. You aren't there yet. You've got five weeks left."

Blair looked glum. "Thanks for reminding me."

Chapter 10

Mark was looking at the calendar. He had noted the day Blair first called Jennifer for a date, according to Robbie. Since then Blair had used up four weeks treating Jennifer to dinners and a play. They went for strolls on the beach and shared ice cream. To Robbie's knowledge, it hadn't gone past the necking stage between Blair and Jennifer. If he called now, Blair wouldn't be prepared. Mark was ninety percent certain she'd agree to see him. After all, they were friends.

"Hello, Jennifer. Is that you?" Mark called from his home.

"Hi, Mark. Haven't heard from you in ages."

"Hey, the B.C. Lions are playing the Calgary Stampeders tonight. Interested?"

"You know I don't know anything about football."

"Sure you do. The object of the game is to –"

"I know that part!" she cut him short.

Mark said, "So you'll go?"

"Okay. But don't you think I'll get bored?"

"You'll be with me. How could you be bored? You need to expose yourself to different things. Think of it as an educational experience."

"We're just friends, right?"

"Sure we are."

She laughed. He arranged to pick her up before kickoff.

They had seats close to the forty-five yard line at B.C. Place. The game didn't hold Jennifer's attention. She kept looking around at the spectators. She asked Mark if they could share some popcorn.

"Sure, if you give me a kiss," he said.

"In front of all these people?" she jested.

"Well, we're on a date, aren't we?"

She put her hands on her hips. "Since when did this turn into a date?"

"Since I asked you for a kiss." He put his arm around her

shoulders.

She pulled away slightly. He sensed her discomfort.

"Mark, what's going on? I didn't know you liked me that way. Are you feeling okay?"

"Do you want to leave and go to my place?"

"Let's just go. You can take me home."

Mark stood up and led her out to the parking lot. He opened the car door for her. She got in and he leaned over and kissed her on the cheek. She averted her eyes and bit down on her lower lip. He got in the driver's seat and drove to his place without a word between them. He turned off the motor and parked.

"Mark, just take me home," she said softly.

"Jennifer, we've been friends a long time, and I've never found anyone as beautiful as you. You're all I want."

He got out and opened her car door. He took her hand and led her to his front door but she refused to go in. He tried one more time. "I want to spend the rest of the evening with you. It's still early. Want to have a coke? There's some in the fridge."

"Mark, you've never ever made overtures to me and suddenly you want me?"

"What's the matter? Are you seeing someone?" asked Mark.

"Actually, yes. This fellow – his name's Blair. I like him and I think he really likes me."

"And I don't? I'm crazy about you. I just never thought you liked me back."

"Mark, I consider you to be my friend." Mark unlocked the door. Jennifer followed him in, continuing the conversation. "I mean I do like you, but as a friend. Don't you see?"

He led her to the sofa. He pulled her close and kissed her forehead, cheeks and lips. She started to yield to his passion. He unbuttoned her blouse. Soon they were at the point of no return. Jennifer swooned and gave into his advances. Afterwards, she drew up her knees and closed her eyes. He held her for a while, and then they got dressed. He offered her a coke, but she declined. He drove her home in silence. He tried to kiss her before she got out of the car. But she nervously chattered about small things and said goodbye hurriedly. She ran up the steps and went in.

Driving back, Mark wondered if he had done the wrong thing. She was so loving, but it was innocence he had taken. She tried to say no, but he thought she wanted it. Did he seduce her just to beat the others at the game?

Robbie exploded after hearing Mark's message on the machine. The recording said simply, "Jennifer has been deflowered." How could this have slipped by under his nose? Jennifer was no longer pure, and Mark was the trophy winner. He called Mark immediately.

"How could this be? Blair had two more weeks. You broke the rules!" Robbie said furiously.

Mark said, "Cool off, Robbie."

"You jumped the gun. So you're the man?" Robbie saw red.

"Listen, I'm taking myself off the list. It's wide open for James."

"You have her, then you ditch her? What kind of man are you? She's yours at least for a second date."

"This isn't meant to be funny. I'm benched. It's over between Jennifer and me. I wouldn't be surprised if she never talks to me again."

"But she was willing, right? No charges will be laid?" said Robbie.

"If it's any consolation to Blair, she did say she liked him."

"Oh, isn't that sweet." Robbie said.

"Don't tell the other guys. Just say I'm out of the game."

"Like you think I can keep a secret?"

Mark said, "She remains unblemished in her heart. She will always be pure."

"So she will choose a life other than prostitution? What have you done?"

"I feel bad enough already. I'm going to get stinking drunk."

Robbie said, "Well, I guess it had to be somebody. Luck of the draw really. Should faze Blair a little, but he'll heal. The others will want to shake your hand."

"Robbie, you have no empathy, do you?"

"For a gigolo like you? No sirree. I'm going to call Blair and then I'm going to call James and down the order."

"Why do you mess with everyone's lives?"

"It's my sworn duty. I hope you sleep well tonight." Robbie hung up and dialed Blair to give him the news.

"I want him arrested," Blair said. He was caught completely off guard. His hands shook he was so upset. This was ugly. Not only did she date another man, but had sex as well. He said to Robbie, "Did he get tested for STDs?"

Surprised at the question, Robbie said, "Not that I know of. I doubt any of us have."

"I did. I had a physical examination, too."

Robbie asked, "Why only you?"

"I think because they didn't figure she'd get serious with any of you in a short period of time. Unfortunately, that wasn't the case."

"Can you find out why we all weren't tested? Just out of curiosity."

"Yeah, then I'm going to hunt Mark down and exterminate him." Blair was angry.

"James is going to be shining his shoes. With Mark out of the picture, he's next."

Dr. Jackson answered a call from an irate Blair Whitman.

"Dr. Jackson, Blair Whitman calling. Do you remember setting up a physical examination and STD testing for me, months back?

"Yes. You were a candidate for the Madame J project."

"Well, she had sexual relations with an untested interloper. Why wasn't he tested? He was one of the six candidates on the list."

"No, there was only one candidate. That's you."

"You must be mistaken. Besides he and I, there are four other potential mates – not to mention if she runs into someone else and things happen."

"What was this fellow's name?" Dr. Jackson pulled a pen out of his chest pocket.

"Mark."

"Last name?"

"Sorry, I don't know his last name."

"Not a lot to go on, but I'll look into it." He wrote down the name and put away the pen.

"Please do."

Dr. Jackson relayed the information to Dr. Hutchinson.

"We overlooked the others because we didn't think it would escalate so quickly in this fashion. Based on Mr. Abrams' advice, we were only dealing with Blair up to this point, because he was the most qualified suitor. We need to take a second look," Dr. Hutchinson said. "At this point, I recommend we do not test the other five. We will just remind them to use prophylactics. Unfortunately, even with meticulous planning, things go awry. That's it for now."

Sean had no idea Jennifer went on a date with Mark until Dr. Hutchinson called him. So much for patient confidentiality. Necessity overruled. These were special circumstances. He said he was surprised that events had unraveled so quickly.

Sean went home that evening very concerned. Jennifer hardly ate anything at dinner. She didn't say a word until Sean asked her a question.

"Say, what have you been up to? More paintings?" he asked.

"I went to a football game," Jennifer said. Mrs. Abrams silently listened to them talk. "It wasn't what I expected."

"You seem a little sad," he said. "Did something happen?"

"I don't really want to talk about it. Let's just say sometimes people do things for the wrong reasons."

Sean said, "What was your reason?"

"I don't know. I'm going to take a bath and go to bed early." She hurriedly cleaned up the dishes and went into her room.

Mrs. Abrams said to him, "She came in last night very distraught. She cried in her room. I'm worried about her."

Sean said, "She'll get over it. Everyone gets over their first time." He squeezed her shoulder.

The next morning at the bank, Blair thought he'd waited long enough to call her. He cracked his knuckles and rehearsed what he wanted to say. His hand was over the receiver when the phone rang.

"Hello, Blair?" Jennifer's voice came over the line. "Can you meet me downstairs? I'm at the diner."

"Ah, sure. Give me ten minutes."

He told his supervisor, he had an emergency and left the

bank. Jennifer sat in a booth by the window. He adjusted his collar and sat down across from her. "What's this urgent meeting about?"

The waitress brought her coffee. He refused ordering. After saying hello, Jennifer said, "I saw a friend of mine. We went to a B.C. Lions game."

"So?"

She shrugged. "We started kissing and one thing led to another. I didn't think about the consequences."

Blair looked at her intensely. She felt remorse. That was a good sign. "What are you trying to say?"

"I'm trying to say I want to maintain our relationship. I don't want to break up because of one indiscretion."

"You slept with someone else? How could you? I thought we had something." Blair couldn't stop the words.

"Yes, and I don't plan on doing it again. I want to be with you."

"Why him? Why now?"

"It's like I grew up overnight. He turned me on. What can I say?"

"I'm angry and disappointed." Blair looked for the right words. "I realize you have a sensitive, trusting nature. We hadn't talked about being exclusive. All I can do is forgive you. Next time you sleep with someone, I hope it's me. I need to get back to work. Call me later."

He rose out of his seat and walked out.

Once outside he realized how jealous he was. It was too late to go back and talk it out. He had work to do. When he got back to his office, he was furious. She had made him a fool.

Later in the day, Blair joined Sean and Charles at the diner. "Am I missing something? Is she going to try us all on for size and play us against each other?"

Charles said, "I remember the day we sat here and she came up with the names. That was the first indication she was attracted to you. I think Sean would agree, in the beginning we never thought she'd move past her relationship with you. We thought it would be clear sailing."

Sean said, "Previously, the others seemed inconsequential. But now we see each of these suitors has potential. They aren't random."

"I disagree. She seems a little confused about whom she wants and what she needs. She's a spider spinning a web catching insects and digesting them. I hate to say it, but what if her motive is experimentation?" said Blair.

Sean disagreed. "Judging by her naiveté, I think she is led by curiosity, not sexual intrigue. If she's planning on a parade of brief interludes, she isn't the daughter I know."

They talked further, but when Blair left, he had no solutions to restrain Jennifer's interest in other men.

Face it, Blair thought to himself. He could not trust that she would make the right decision if she were propositioned by any of the remaining choices. If he tried to corral her, it might lead to resistance and push her into another's arms. He could ask her to promise to be exclusive in their relationship, but impulses could still pull her in the opposite direction.

He hung onto the fact that she and he had such a good relationship up until now. If he bowed out, he'd lose out on being part of the inner circle and a possible wonderful marriage to Jennifer. But he could only be pushed so far.

The other question was, why did Mark bow out after having sex with her?

Chapter 11

James got out his best shirt, shaved and went to the mental health team with the intention of running into Jennifer. He knew her regular visits were the first Wednesday of the month at two o'clock. He had been preparing since he got the call that Mark had removed himself from the race. He thought the whole idea of waiting was absurd. He was up for it. He decided he'd try his own angle.

Jennifer walked in at two o'clock sharp. She was wearing a navy polka dot outfit. The print made his eyes swim. He smiled at her. "Hi, how are you, Jennifer?"

She sat down next to him in the waiting area. "Fine, James. Do you have an appointment?"

He casually leaned forward. "Yeah. You want to get together afterwards? I thought you might like to see my latest paintings. They're showing at a coffee shop five minutes from here. Interested?"

"Yes, I'd like to see them."

James waited for half an hour for Jennifer to come out of her meeting. He didn't have an appointment; it was only a white lie. She came out and said, "Are you ready to go?"

They walked down the street toward the coffee shop. Jennifer started to feel a little anxious. She felt attracted to his good looks. He didn't say anything along the way. Nervously, she said, "How many paintings do you have there?"

"You'll see." There was an uncomfortable silence. They got to the coffee shop and he opened the door for her. The place was air-conditioned. They each paid for their own iced coffee and sat down. She felt a little tongue-tied. She didn't know what to say. All of sudden she felt very shy. He also seemed unusually quiet. He stared at his cup and studied the pattern on the wood tabletop. He fiddled with his pack of cigarettes, but it was a smoke-free environment.

She gazed around at the multitude of paintings. "Are these all yours?"

"The ones on the north wall are mine. The other artists I don't know."

"So, do you use acrylics?"

"Mixed media."

"I quite like the one on the far left. I've never seen anything like it."

"Thanks." They sat in silence drinking their iced coffees. After a pause, he said, "It's hard to say, but I really like you." He made eye contact.

Politely, she said, "Oh, I like you, too."

"I mean I really like you." His expression got warm and soft.

"James, I don't know what to say. I think you are a real nice guy but –"

"What? My hair's too short? I'm too young. I'm not good enough for you." Suddenly his attitude changed.

"No, I wasn't going to say that. I was going to say I'm seeing this guy."

"Oh, is he rich and famous?"

"He's not better than you," Jennifer said.

"Then why not us? Why can't we be together? I've got a place. You could move in. We could –"

"Hold your horses! What's with men in my life these days? Has the world gone mad?"

James grinned. "I think the general consensus is you're the prize."

"Whom have you been talking to? I don't believe this. It's like a date conspiracy."

James howled. "You've become very popular all of a sudden. You're with different guys every night. It's like the flavour of the week, isn't it?"

"How do you know I've been dating different guys?" Jennifer gasped.

"I have my sources. I think you're an angel from heaven."

Jennifer was embarrassed. "You floor me."

"And vice versa."

She took a breath. "I'm in deep water up to my neck. Can we just slow down here?"

"I'm saying what's on my mind. I could fall in love with you."

"Quite honestly, I don't want to go there."

James put his cup aside and put his hand over her fingers on the table. "What's stopping you? It's a free country. You don't have to live by anyone's rules except your own. People fall in and out of love everyday. Why can't we try? Otherwise, we'll never know."

"Maybe I'm not the one for you. It's complicated."

"It doesn't have to be. Go with the feeling."

"You really are more than I can handle right now. My boyfriend is considerate and polite. Our relationship is rocky right now. He's not going to forgive me if I start up with you." She pulled her hand away.

"Cross that bridge when you come to it. Incidentally, 'polite' isn't actually how you'd describe someone you are in love with."

"I'm only starting to know him. He takes it pretty slow."

"Maybe it's too slow. Maybe you need action rather than words," James said. He gently touched her knee under the table.

She giggled. "Cut that out!" She relaxed a little and said, "He'd never do that with me."

"Sounds like he's staid. You could have a lot more fun with me. We could go to clubs and concerts."

"There you go, dreaming again. I'm not certain I want to pursue this." She rolled her eyes.

"Let me pursue you." His hand reached out to grab her under the table.

"Stop touching my knee!" she yelped. The couple at the next table glanced over. Embarrassed, she said, "Let's go." They got up and left.

Standing outside the coffee shop, she said, "I think you paint from your heart." They locked gazes and he put his hand on the back of her neck. Soon they were in a clinch. She came up for a breather. "Whew. You're a good kisser."

He kissed her again.

Jennifer opened her eyes and checked her watch. "Sorry, I've got to leave." She turned and walked down the street in the direction they came from.

James spotted Robbie in sunglasses across the street leaning on a mailbox. Robbie crossed the street and joined James. Previously, James told him about his plan to meet Jennifer at the mental health team. It didn't surprise him that Robbie was there. Robbie was a voyeur; that was true. He knew any goings-on he had with Jennifer would be communicated to Blair through Robbie. James expected Blair would act quickly. He knew the rules Blair abided by were different than his own. James took what was available; Blair stood on propriety. Mark had a one-nighter with her. Now it was his opportunity to be with her next.

"Where's your binoculars, Robbie?" said James. "You've got to work on your spying technique. I could see you the whole time."

"More importantly, she didn't. Got a light?" James flicked his lighter and Robbie held his cigarette to the flame. "How was it?" James lit his own cigarette.

"The kiss you mean? It was a three out of four."

"Why only three?"

"Because we had to stop," James said.

"Are you going to see her again soon?"

"I'll find a way," James said. "Love begins as a spur of the moment kind of thing. I think Blair's going to get another rude awakening he's not the be-all and end-all. He'll get a run for his money."

"Geez, how could any one man hold her? She's way too free with her affections. The bus driver, the mailman could be next. She's out of control."

"She's not that. She's just untying her tightly wound self. Before she wouldn't even look me in the eye. I'd say she's bolder than she's ever been."

"Well, in six weeks I get the chance of a lifetime." Robbie patted his chest.

"You're so hyped up. I bet you don't get to first base," James replied.

"And why wouldn't I?"

"Because you left your libido in the freezer. You talk so much about what you want, but you never acted on impulse to approach her. She doesn't see you spying on her because she probably doesn't even know what you look like since high school. I'm telling you as a friend, the apple is ready to be picked. I don't really care if she dumps me. At this point, I'm just glad she responded the way she did. In the long term, I know this thing with her won't last. She's like water, and I'm swimming in it now. But at the end of the day, we all go home."

"You're giving up? You don't want to make it permanent with Jennifer?" said Robbie.

"I realize she's her own person and I can't fulfill all her needs. I think Blair's the one for her. I can't afford her. Besides, she needs someone more stable than me. It could be very stormy for her and me. Can you imagine us both tripping into delusions at the same time?"

"I never thought about that. I can be obsessive and get angry too." Robbie thought for a moment. "Geezus, I wish I could be you right now."

"I know how you feel about her, but you can't reach her by sitting on your ass. You need to keep your emotions in check if you want to get close to her. She's delicate. If she sees you as a predator, it's goodbye."

"How do you know so much?"

"Because I've met a lot of different types of women, but they all respond to openness and flattery. Are you ready to take a flying leap?" James flicked his cigarette and crushed the butt with his leather shoe.

James didn't contact Jennifer. He had left it open with no concrete plans. She didn't have his phone number or any way of contacting him. He decided maybe he'd just let it go. She was sweet and all that, but his feelings toward her burned off pretty quickly when he thought about Robbie's dilemma. Robbie would carry his love to the grave, if he didn't do something about it now.

Blair had repeat calls from Robbie, but didn't phone him back. Robbie was a nuisance.

Jennifer had called him a few times to patch things up. He was still sore but willing to see her again. There was a lot at stake.

Blair left work and drove to Jennifer's house. They had arranged to have pizza together at his place. She waited for him, swinging back and forth on the porch swing. He parked out front. Happily, she jumped off the porch swing and into the car.

Jennifer talked nonstop in the car and up the elevator. Seeing his place for the first time made her animated. When they entered his condo, she said, "Wow, what a nice place. The décor is fabulous. Do you think one of my paintings could go there?" She pointed above the couch.

"Let me show you the bedroom. It's done in taupe and black." He opened the door to a cozy room dimly lit by track lighting. On the bed was a negligee.

Jennifer looked at him coyly. "Whom does that belong to?"

"It's for you." He leaned close and kissed her. He unbuttoned her blouse and exposed her satin bra. He kissed her again, running his fingers along the edge of her bra. He started to unzip her jeans. She pulled away slightly. "Let me make love to you. I want this first time together to be special." He leaned forward and engulfed her.

In the throes of heightened excitement, she called out, "I love you, James."

Blair immediately froze. "What did you call me?"

"I called you Blair, didn't I?"

Blair backed off. "No, you called me James." He pulled away from her and sat on the edge of the bed.

"It was a slip of the tongue. I meant to call you Blair." She placed her fingers on his shoulders and started to massage his muscles.

"Who's James?"

"James? I don't know a James."

"You're lying."

"He's an acquaintance of mine."

Blair said, "An acquaintance you've made love to recently?"

"We went for coffee and he kissed me. That's all. I wasn't going to say, because I didn't want to hurt your feelings."

"I thought you wanted me." Blair sounded angry.

"I didn't sleep with James. I haven't seen or heard from him since."

Blair seethed. "I see you aren't mature enough for this relationship. We're terminated. I'll give you the pizza, and you can go home."

"I don't care about the pizza. I care about you!"

"I can't trust you! You hurt me more than you know."

"I'm sorry. What can I say?"

"Are you hiding behind an excuse of vulnerability? You calculated this from the start. I know you have a list," he blurted out.

Jennifer gasped. "A list? What list?" Then the truth dawned on her. She remembered the conversation with her father and Charles Groder. She said, "Now I remember. I see it so clearly. You're all competing for me. My dad asked me how I would choose a husband and I came up with that list. It was to be taken lightly, not turn into an ugly battle. I promptly forgot about it."

"So which of these six suitors do you really want? Because I'm not going to sit here while you flip a coin."

"Good grief. The six were just six men I knew. I'm not a tramp or a vamp. I was just making conversation."

"You and your feminine wiles. Do you know what you've done? This isn't a game. This is reality."

"So you think I'm wicked?"

The conversation frazzled Blair. "What about the Valentine's Day card? Do you remember that?" He started to put his clothes back on. She did the same.

"Can you refresh my memory?" She buttoned her blouse.

Wordlessly, he reached into the drawer of his bedside table and passed her the envelope containing the card. She looked at the hearts and the message. She knew she had pushed him to the limit: first the card, then the list, sleeping with Mark and kissing James. She saw how far Blair had come to be with her now. He really had gone all out for her; and she in return had cheated him and played him to be the fool. She realized his love was deeper than she had imagined. He was really a gentleman all through their relationship and she had repaid him with hurt and confusion.

"Blair, now that I know, I want to be clear there is no one between us. I know I've made mistakes, but I love you."

"Think of the others on the list. Do any of the others stand a chance with you? No matter how small or large, I need to know."

"Well, there's Mark. I don't want to see him again. There's James. He's cute and all, but he's so young. Then there's –" Suddenly she froze.

"What is it?" Blair asked.

"Oh my god. Robbie's next!"

The rest of the evening didn't go that well for Blair. Jennifer's pupils dilated at the mention of Robbie's name. She really took the cake when it got right down to it. How could she be so fickle? She actually sat on the bed, talking about how much she loved Robbie as a teenager. She totally disregarded his feelings. He sat there pretending to pay attention while she told her tale.

"What the hell does he mean to you a decade later? You don't know his present circumstances or even have a remote idea where or who he is today. He's not the person that you idealize him to be. He's a stranger, Jen. Live in the present. He's wrong for you. Honestly." Blair threw the words at her.

Jennifer pondered as she took the bus home. Blair didn't volunteer to give her a ride.

They both had a lot of thinking to do.

Chapter 12

The next day, James called Robbie. "I'm officially withdrawing because I feel you need to speak to Jennifer. It's your turn. Good luck."

Robbie hung up the phone. He drove to her house. When he got there, he sat in the car fidgeting. Finally, he got out of the car. At the same moment, she opened the door to let the cat out.

He waved and grinned. "Is that you, Jennifer?" He walked along the concrete sidewalk to her front stoop.

With a puzzled look, she asked, "Do I know you?" She came out onto the porch. He ran up the last couple of steps.

"It's me Robbie."

"Robbie Heedes? Is it really you?" She looked stunned.

"I've been wanting to speak with you, but I never had the chance."

"It's been a long time since high school. How have you been?"

"I never completed high school. I started out waiting tables, then moved to restaurant management. You seem different, a little older and wiser." She smiled. Taking a breath, he asked, "Do you think we could go out sometime? Catch a movie?"

She looked at him and boldly said, "You want to know something? There was a time I'd travel to the moon just to be with you. The image of you gave me something to aim for during a difficult time in my life. But now, I think I have to say no. People change, ideals change, emotions change."

"There's no chance between us?"

"I loved you once. I think closure is all I want now. Just to say what I've said and start anew."

Robbie said, "Thank you for saying that. I couldn't say it any better than you. So many times I wanted to contact you, but was unable to do so. If I think real hard I can see how our paths crossed, diverged and crossed again. Hopefully, I will see you again. Perhaps when you become a famous writer."

"What are you talking about? I'm not a famous writer."

"Let's just say, I knew you in school and boy, could you write. I saw some of your poems on the English teacher's desk."

"Hold on. Are you saying I wrote poetry in the past? I don't remember."

"Well, those poems became popular songs, successful ones. Of course you know that?"

"Actually, no. This is the first time someone's told me that I was a bona fide writer. This is the first proof I've had that points in that direction. For some reason I believe you! Thank you so much. Now I can really believe in myself. I have this incredible feeling. It's like a huge boulder was pinning me down, and you rolled it away."

Robbie said, "Can I say one more thing?"

"Certainly."

"I could help you become a writer for Hollywood. I know you had the ability to write stories in the past. Not just any old stories, but really fascinating ones. I can help you make connections in Hollywood. Give me the opportunity to help you."

Jennifer replied, "My writing has been affected by illness. I don't know if I could pull it off. Could I call you when I had something I thought was good enough?"

"Sure, here's my card." He handed her a business card. He took her hand and squeezed it. "I think this is the beginning of a beautiful friendship."

"*Casablanca*, 1943," she said. "Thanks. I'll keep your number in a safe place."

Jennifer began to write with renewed fervor. She didn't remember how to write lyrics anymore. Instead she attempted to write scripts in the same style as the movies she admired. Her writing was more sophisticated and in depth than anything she had accomplished before. She studied books on writing and enrolled in a film school.

To those who knew Jennifer it was clear she was in love with Blair. Bill and Chris withdrew. When Blair asked her to move in, she was very pleased. She chose him because of their common values and personalities. He said he chose her simply because he loved her. After she unpacked, she hung her pictures, set up her easel and settled in.

Dr. Hutchinson was on the phone to Sean. He was very excited, which didn't happen often. He said, "She's gone into complete remission. I directed her to taper off her medication to zero."

"What made this possible?" Sean asked.

"It started with her visit from Robbie Heedes. He opened the door, so to speak."

"I thought they'd never get together on any level," said Sean.

"As part of the study, we barred her from being recognized for her writing. This component created an imbalance that contributed to her low self-esteem and paranoid thoughts necessary for to the study. Unfortunately, lack of recognition also hindered her recovery. It was a double-edged sword. She could never even out because she was missing a huge chunk out of her life. She developed amnesia about her accomplishments soon after she got ill. Robbie was part of that missing piece."

"How did she receive the news that she was a government experiment? Really, if she had that information earlier, she could have been cured years ago."

"She was ready to declare war until I played her the tape about it being her idea. She didn't have a leg to stand on, once she realized she had brought it upon herself. Even if she wanted to sue, it would destroy her to go to trial and be questioned on the stand. Once it was confirmed that she had written all those songs, she was happier than a clam. Any resentment she felt was mostly erased. People have been taking care of her for years, finding suitable singers and producing her songs."

"And her relationship with Robbie?"

"They're getting along fine. They're flying to Los Angeles to meet with a director."

"Do you think she'll be successful? Screenwriting is a tough business."

"I'm sure they will all be lined up based on her public talent."

"Public talent?" said Sean.

"For years, Robbie's been spreading the news that the ghostwriter of the century was none other than Miss Jennifer Abrams. He's going to take care of her. You wait and see. It's going to be a victory for Jennifer when that comes out."

"The contracts I made on her behalf state she can't go public with her ghostwriting of individual songs. A general statement to the press without naming names, however, is fine."

"I wish the best for her."

"By the way, Blair proposed to Jennifer. They set a date for next May," Sean said.

"Wonderful for you to tell me, but I already knew that," said Dr. Hutchinson. "Another positive thing came out of this."

"What's that?" Sean asked.

"During her illness she offered us a lot of information about schizophrenia. We know more about the illness and how the mind works than ever before. We studied and researched many cases of schizophrenia since the time our project began. We used her as a model for us to track and develop better ways to aid other mentally ill persons. It's notable that success cured her in a way. The fact she finally knew the truth and her contribution to society was the main factor in her recovery. To compensate for pain and suffering and the information we gleaned from her, we are going to reward her with ten million dollars in a lump sum payment. How does that grab you?"

Sean whistled.

"She got the maximum the government could afford," said Dr. Hutchinson.

"I've also got a trust fund for her based on royalties from her writing. Well, I guess I don't have to worry about Jennifer anymore."

"Nor I. We'll watch her, but she may not need it. With the information we have now, we can move forward and improve treatment and services. With this project alone, we have accelerated our scientific knowledge in leaps and bounds."

"And a cure? Did the growth hormone work?" asked Sean.

"No, but it did make her taller."

"Say, if you ever need a lawyer..."

"I know. You're on my list."

From New York to Vancouver : stories on

CPSIA information can be obtained
at www.ICGtesting.com
Printed in the USA
LVHW041928010922
727394LV00002B/277

9 781979 805346